PRACTICAL SCHOOLING

PRACTICAL SCHOOLING

IMPROVING THE HORSE AND RIDER

Michael J. Stevens

KENILWORTH PRESS

First published in Great Britain 1995 by
The Kenilworth Press Ltd
Addington
Buckingham
MK18 2JR

British Library Cataloguing in Publication Data
A CIP record for this book is available from the British Library

ISBN 1-872082-76-9

Computer-generated drawings by the author
Line illustrations by Dianne Breeze
Cover design by Paul Saunders
Typeset in 11.5/13 Goudy
Design, typesetting and layout by The Kenilworth Press Ltd
Printed and bound in Great Britain by
Butler and Tanner Ltd, Frome

CONTENTS

PREFACE

My aim in presenting this guide is to encourage all horse owners to spend more time schooling their horses. Many riders feel they ought to work in the school but seldom get around to it. I particularly want to persuade these riders to try their hand at schooling, as I am certain the results will make all their efforts worthwhile. Schooling provides an effective means of improving our horses, and it cultivates our own skills in the saddle. Our endeavours are inevitably rewarded with a more enjoyable riding experience both for ourselves and for our horses.

Properly organised schooling is very good for horses, both physically and mentally. The exercise does the same for them as participation in a sporting activity does for us. Hacking out has little more beneficial effect on them than a gentle stroll about has on us. In addition to all the benefits of physical exercise, if we plan the schooling sensibly we can make our horses more supple, more responsive, and easier to ride. We can improve their mental composure, keeping them calm, whilst at the same time improving their learning capabilities. As a result we can enable them to perform far better than we had ever imagined possible.

I have provided here all the information the rider will need in order to make a start. The guide can be used as a source of information for those who work alone, or it can be treated as a reference book to complement practical sessions under the supervision of a coach.

The material contained herein is based both on my studies of classical riding and on my experiences over the years of trying to improve, by schooling, a large number of very ordinary horses and ponies. The majority of these never had the benefit of a good basic training, and in consequence many of them presented difficulties of one sort or another which had to be overcome. I have devoted a substantial section of the book to dealing with common problems.

Some riders are hesitant about venturing into the manege because they are not really sure what they should do when they get there. Others do not have a clear idea of how to set about achieving their objectives. I hope this book will provide some of the answers to these questions, and I hope it will generate a greater enthusiasm for school riding in the equestrian community at large.

Michael J Stevens
August 1995

ACKNOWLEDGEMENTS

I would like to acknowledge the Training the Teachers of Tomorrow Trust, who provide regular opportunities for studying classical horsemanship. Without this organisation I should have been ill prepared for applying classical methods to the schooling of ordinary horses, and this book could not have been contemplated.

Stella Vincent put a lot of time and effort into correcting my original manuscript, and made a valuable contribution in suggesting a number of improvements. I am most grateful for her assistance.

I am delighted with the marvellous illustrations penned by Dianne Breeze. They add enormously to the visual impact, and I am indebted to her for all the trouble she took.

Particular thanks are due to Lesley Gowers, managing editor, who has expertly overseen all stages of production from rough draft to final publication. All credit for the excellent layout and design lies with Rachel Howe.

INTRODUCTION

As everyone knows, you cannot take a young horse and expect to have a good ride straight away; he needs to be trained first. Similarly you will not be rewarded with a perfect ride on an older horse unless he is given some revision schooling from time to time. In practice it is rather difficult to distinguish between riding and schooling, because everything we do with our horses has some effect on them, either for better or for worse. Schooling could perhaps be defined as riding in a way which is calculated to have a beneficial long term effect. No true horseman will fully enjoy his time with horses unless he takes an active interest in this process of schooling.

Being a versatile creature, the horse is capable of serving us in various ways. He is eminently trainable, and within the limits imposed by nature we can develop his latent talents according to our requirements, to suit our differing needs.

Different groups of people train their horses in different ways. Many riding school proprietors do not school their horses at all. They are content to provide animals that will carry the weekend rider safely around the countryside for a little exercise. It is on animals such as these that most of us with a more educated interest in riding are also obliged to learn, and indeed it is upon such horses that our teachers are usually trained. This is an unfortunate state of affairs, because the horses generally are not physically or mentally relaxed, and few of them are capable of responding correctly to the aids. Experiences gained on such horses are largely irrelevant to the art of riding. Although we English love our horses we do not really take their schooling seriously.

Eventers miss half the fun of riding because they do not know how to collect their horses. When they venture into the manege they are often in such a hurry that they look as if they would need three circuits to stop! Show jumpers like their horses to negotiate corners by leaning onto the inside shoulder and bending their necks around to the outside. Some of them have to use strong bits to stay in control. Dressage riders like their horses to move energetically forwards and they want them to flex at the poll. They often pursue these aims even if it means sacrificing lightness and relaxation.

Away from competitive pressures, the average rider loves his horse dearly, hopes he will stay fit and well for many a long year, and wants him to be calm and easy to ride. The modern equestrian shares these quite reasonable demands with all the classical riding masters of the past. Happily the schooling methods that were developed by these venerable horsemen have survived the passage of time. They are available to us today, and they are just as relevant now as they were hundreds of years ago.

The classical approach to schooling provides a proved, systematic, and civilised procedure for developing the horse's natural abilities so that he can enjoy his life to the full whilst becoming all that any normal horseman could desire in a good riding horse. You can observe the horses produced by the show jumpers, eventers, and dressage riders at any top level competition in each of their specialist fields. If you want to see what can be achieved with classical riding then watch a performance of the Spanish Riding School of Vienna, and you will have no doubt in your mind as to which is the best doctrine to follow.

To be a successful rider it is not necessary to be famous or to compete at important horse shows. It is essential, however, to be patient and understanding, and to have a tenacious desire to reach your goals. These are qualities which, if they are not in your nature, you will find very difficult to learn, but if you are an enthusiastic equestrian you should have no trouble in gaining the additional knowledge and skills which will enable you to become a good rider. You must know how to sit correctly and how to use your body, legs and arms to explain your wishes to the horse, and you need to know what equipment to use. You must be able to recognise when the horse is going well, and when he is going badly. You must always have clear schooling objectives in mind and you must know how these can be attained. When problems arise you must be able to solve them effectively without offending the principles of classical horsemanship, which demand that you try to understand the horse's difficulties and do not act rashly or resort to force.

Some riders believe that their horses do not enjoy school work. In fact the manege offers scope for such a variety of patterns and exercises that no horse will ever be bored. It is certainly more interesting than going out regularly on the same few rides and always trotting or cantering at the same point on the route! More often it is the riders themselves who find schooling dull, usually because they do not know how to proceed, or because they are unsure how to select and apply appropriate exercises for making the improvements they hope to establish.

After a little schooling remarkable improvements can be made to many horses. Do you always have to ride a trot before you can move into canter? You can probably teach your horse to canter directly from a walk; and a more pleasant canter it will be too. At the end of a canter do you always get a harsh jolting trot? Do you have to pull hard to stop? Does your horse jog instead of walking? You will be able to handle all these problems and more besides, once you develop an interest in schooling.

If you really get the schooling 'bug', then in time your horse will improve out of all recognition. He will always be pleasant to ride, and who knows, you might one day be able to perform some of the advanced exercises that are demanded at Grand Prix level dressage.

TERMINOLOGY

This section defines some of the terms from the language of riding which are employed in this book:

When the horse is bent laterally in either direction he is described as having an *inside* and an *outside*. When he is bent to the right, for example, his right side is the inside. This remains true regardless of the direction in which he is going, or his whereabouts in the manege.

Collection is the way a horse carries himself when he bends the joints of his hindlegs and takes more weight on his haunches. The collected horse is ready to obey his rider's commands at a moment's notice.

Cadence is the description applied to a gait when the steps become more lofty and suspended. This usually occurs during collection.

Extension is a lengthening of the strides so that at each step the horse covers more ground.

Lightness is that very desirable quality exhibited by the well trained horse which renders him responsive to the seat, leg, and rein aids so that the rider is not obliged to exert himself.

A horse is **well balanced** when he is easy to manœuvre, can sustain his present rate without increasing his speed, and can be brought to rest effortlessly.

The **rhythm** of a gait is correct when every stride is completed in an equal period of time.

Impulsion is the force which drives the horse onwards. If a horse lacks impulsion it is difficult to make him extend the gait or change to a faster gait.

Engagement is the term used to describe the action of a hind limb when it steps well forwards under the horse's body so that it is in a good position to lift and propel the horse along.

The horse is said to be **on the forehand**

when he carries his weight too much on his shoulders and too little on his haunches. He is **on the haunches** when he takes the weight back on all the joints of his hind legs.

If the horse is turning to the right and produces a left lead canter, or is turning to the left and produces a right lead canter he is said to be in a **false canter**. When, as a schooling exercise, the rider deliberately asks the horse to lead with the leg opposite to the direction of the turn, the gait is known as a **counter-canter**.

The horse can be ridden either on a **single track** or **laterally** on **two tracks**. In single track work his hind feet follow in the track made by his fore feet. In two track work the horse moves laterally at an angle to the direction he is facing, so that his hind feet make a separate track on the ground. Lateral movements are ridden because of their value as gymnastic exercises.

Shoulder-in is a lateral movement in which the shoulders are brought in away from the track that the haunches are on. The hind feet move on one track, and the forefeet move on an inner track.

Haunches-in is a lateral exercise in which the haunches are brought in away from the track that the shoulders are on. The forefeet move on one track, and the hind feet move on an inner track.

The **half-pass** is a two track exercise in which the horse progresses diagonally forwards and sideways.

The **simple change** of lead at canter is a method of changing from a left lead canter to a right lead canter, or vice versa. It is effected by changing down directly from canter to walk and then striking off into canter on the opposite lead after two or three steps of walk.

The **flying change** is a method that can be employed by the advanced horse to change the lead at canter. He changes from one lead to the other in mid air without having to change down to another gait first.

The **piaffe** and the **passage** are variations of the trot for the advanced horse. The piaffe is a highly collected movement in which the horse marks time on the spot, moving his legs diagonally as in the trot. The passage is a spectacular lofty floating trot which appears to be executed in slow motion.

At the **pirouette**, which can be performed at the walk, canter, or piaffe, the horse performs a 360° turn around his inside hind foot. When starting from a halt and practised at the walk, this exercise is known as a **turn on the haunches**. Only an advanced horse will be able to produce the pirouette at the canter and at the piaffe.

The **school jumps** are practised by particularly talented horses that have been fully trained in the art of classical riding. There are a number of variations, in which the horse jumps up into the air without the assistance of an obstacle over which to leap. These jumps are regularly demonstrated by the Lipizzaner stallions at the Spanish Riding School in Vienna.

1

THE NATURAL GAITS OF THE HORSE

The walk

At the walk the horse has either two or three feet on the ground at any one time. When he starts to reach forward with his right foreleg the other three feet will be on the ground. As he continues stretching this leg forwards he lifts up his left hindfoot, which leaves his right hind and left fore as the only two feet on the ground. Next he sets down his right forefoot in its new position.

The left hindleg continues to move forwards, and just before the foot is placed on the ground the left forefoot is raised, so that for a moment the horse is supported only by his right hind and right fore legs. The left foreleg continues to reach forwards and the sequence continues as a mirror image of the first part of the stride when the right fore was moving forwards. Now the right hind is the next foot to be lifted.

You should notice four distinct footfalls:

left hind, left fore, right hind, right fore, repeated in quick succession.

The trot

When trotting, the horse has either two feet on the ground or none at all. He springs from one diagonally opposite pair of legs to the other, with a so called 'period of suspension' in between.

You should notice two distinct footfalls at every stride: left hind and right fore together, followed by right hind and left fore together.

The canter

As the horse bounds along at canter he has successively one, three, two, three, one, and finally, for a brief moment, no feet at all on the ground. For a right lead canter the sequence starts with the left hindfoot being placed on the ground. Then the left

The sequence of steps at the walk

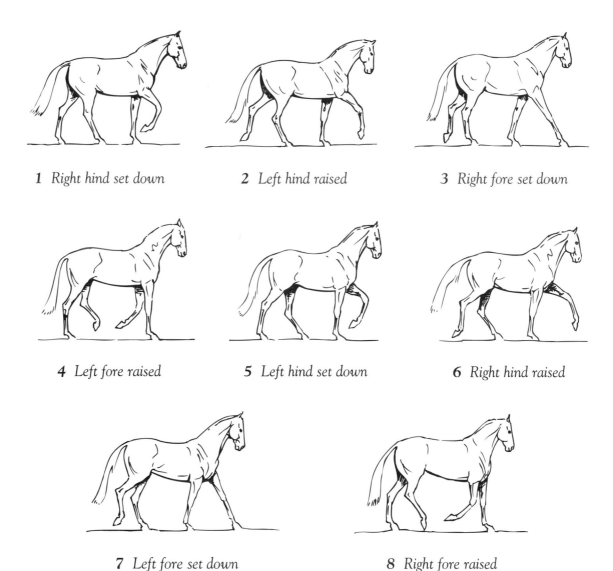

1 *Right hind set down*   **2** *Left hind raised*   **3** *Right fore set down*

4 *Left fore raised*   **5** *Left hind set down*   **6** *Right hind raised*

7 *Left fore set down*   **8** *Right fore raised*

fore and the right hind are set down together. As the horse stretches forwards he lifts his left hind and reaches out with his right fore, which he places on the ground. He then lifts the left diagonal pair of legs so that he is supported only by his right foreleg. As this leg passes beyond the vertical, an upthrust from the foot lifts the horse into a short period of suspension. The next stride begins as the left hindfoot reaches forwards and touches down on the ground again.

You should notice three distinct footfalls,

left hind, left fore and right hind together, and finally the right fore, following one another very quickly, and separated from the next stride by a short delay, a small part of which is taken up by the period of suspension.

Because there are three footfalls, the canter is often said to be a three beat gait. This is not strictly true. In terms of a musical analogy it is really a four beat gait, the three footfalls each corresponding to a played note, and the delay corresponding to a rest.

Suspension at trot and canter

Recent observations from a video recording of Olympic dressage horses, played back in slow motion, revealed that the percentage time occupied by the period of suspension at trot and canter was:

Collected canter	12.5%
Extended canter	18.8%
Collected trot	33.3%
Extended trot	50.0%

Suspension at canter is noticeably less than

The sequence of steps at the trot

1 *The horse springs from the left diagonal...*

2 *...into suspension with the right diagonal advancing...*

3 *...lands on and springs from the right diagonal...*

4 *...into suspension with the left diagonal advancing.*

The sequence of steps at the canter (right lead)

1 *Left hind set down*

2 *Left diagonal set down*

3 *Left hind raised*

4 *Right fore set down*

5 *Left diagonal raised*

6 *Right fore raised*

that at the trot, which probably explains why the canter is easier to sit to than the trot. At the extended trot the horse spends half the time in mid air.

Variations within the gaits

The horse can walk, trot, or canter in many different ways. Sometimes he collects himself together and moves slowly and gracefully, and at others he moves energetically, covering a tremendous amount of ground at each stride. In between these extremes he can vary the cadence, collection, and impulsion to produce infinite nuances of the same gait. In modern dressage tests several variations of gait must be shown, and the horse must change distinctly from one to another. By convention certain varieties of gait are given descriptive names:

Ordinary

The gait the horse will normally choose if he is left alone and the rider does not try to influence him. Not at all eye catching, and rather boring to look at. Convenient for travelling, and adequate as gentle exercise, but having limited gymnastic potential. Working the horse at the ordinary gaits does not have any significant impact on his physical development.

The term *ordinary* has almost fallen into disuse, probably because the ordinary gaits do not constitute a schooling objective, but rather they are an accidental result of a lack of schooling or a lack of proper influence over the horse. Nevertheless it still provides a good description of the gaits of an unschooled horse. If you usually hack out with your horse and you are only just starting to take an interest in schooling then almost certainly you will have been riding the ordinary gaits up until now. Now is the time to learn to ride some of the other variations.

Working

A more controlled gait, generally employed only at the trot or the canter, which shows the beginnings of collection: the horse takes a little more weight on his hindquarters. This variation is ideal for use in the riding school. It is suitable for riding the school patterns, and as such it provides a useful basis for gymnastic exercise. Working gaits are generally reserved for use with young horses, because they are inferior to the collected gaits, which should be used in preference as soon as the horse can master them. You should never aim to ride the working gaits: you should always aim for collection, but until the horse is sufficiently experienced the working gaits will temporarily represent the limit of his capability.

Collected

When working in collection the horse will take noticeably more weight on his haunches. He will move with slightly higher steps, and become more proud and beautiful in his bearing. He will cover less ground at each step than he did at the working gaits. The contact with the bit will be pleasantly light at all times, and you will be able to ride smaller more intricate school patterns. Your control of the horse will be more effective in collection, and this makes it particularly valuable for schooling. The collected walk is one of the most difficult gaits to obtain. Only a well trained horse will be able to perform this successfully.

Medium

At the medium gaits the horse moves more vigorously, thrusting himself forwards with active hind limbs. His frame lengthens a little and he covers more ground at each stride than he does at the collected or working gaits. As with the collected gaits he takes slightly loftier steps than at the working gaits.

Extended

The extended gaits represent the limit of the horse's capacity for travelling energetically forwards. Bringing his hip joints into play he propels himself forwards, covering as much ground at each stride as he possibly can. As with the medium gaits he lengthens his frame a little too. At the extended trot, as each foreleg stretches forward, there will be a moment when it is held out perfectly straight, and the whole picture will look very impressive. Trot and canter extensions should not be practised on hard ground, as the concussion to the horse's feet would be too great.

Free

Here the horse is allowed to stretch his head and neck forwards and down, to lengthen his frame, relax, and swing his back. The free walk should be used as a reward and as a break from intensive work. The free trot and canter can be used as a test to check that the horse is using his back properly and is stretching to seek the guidance of the bit.

School

The school gaits are available only to the advanced school horse. The horse is collected beyond the level that he displays at the collected gaits. The main advantage of increasing the collection to this level is that the rider is then better able to make minor adjustments to the horse's way of going, so that his ability to school the horse is enhanced.

The school trot paves the way for the piaffe and the passage. At the school canter the horse travels at a man's walking rate. This is the canter that the advanced rider will use when executing the pirouette. In former times much use was made of the school walk, but it is seldom practised these days. When the walk is collected to this degree the gait changes, and the horse moves diagonally opposite legs together. The gait becomes more like a gentle trot without a period of suspension. Today such a walk would be penalised as a fault if it were shown in a dressage competition.

Although the term *school* in the context of the gaits is well understood in classical circles, it is not generally employed in other branches of horse riding.

2

SCHOOLING OBJECTIVES

Before starting to school our horses we must have some overall objectives in mind. For their sakes we want them to be fit and strong so that they can cope with their work easily and have a long stress-free working life, and for our own convenience we want to train them so they are easy to ride.

We want them to look proud and beautiful, and we want them to be supple, relaxed, and gentle in their action so that their movements are comfortable to sit to. We want them to be light to the aids so they move willingly without our having to exert ourselves unduly, and naturally we want to be able to stop them easily too. We would also like them to be equally easy to turn to the left and to the right.

One of the most important goals is to increase the amount of weight that the horse carries on his haunches, which will at the same time lighten the burden he takes on his shoulders. This will make him far more manoeuvrable and will go a long way towards satisfying our quest for a better ride.

From an observer's point of view there are a number of signs that good riders and well schooled horses invariably exhibit. Never confuse these signs with the primary aims of schooling. For example, a well balanced horse who uses his back properly and engages his hindlegs will naturally round his neck and flex at the poll. Some riders make the mistake of forcing the horse into this ideal shape instead of concentrating on the basic objective and teaching him to take the weight back to cultivate his balance and posture. You can certainly make the horse flex at the poll if that is what you really want to do. You might even fool an observer or an inexperienced judge into thinking the horse is well schooled, because superficially he will look quite attractive. Unfortunately he will not be any better to ride, because making him flex in this way will not help him to engage his hindlegs, and thus he will remain uncollected and unbalanced.

One must always be very careful not to jump to conclusions when interpreting the various signs of good or bad riding. If the horse tosses his head about it could be that he has not learned to seek a contact with the bit, or it might be that the rider has harsh hands. When the horse shakes his head because he is worried by flies, however, there is nothing intrinsically wrong with him or his training; he is just behaving normally, and neither you nor an experienced judge should have any cause to be displeased with him.

Purity of the gaits

When riding the horse we should always allow him to move as nature intended, and to this end we must ensure that his natural gaits are kept absolutely pure. He must always maintain the sequence of steps that are dictated by nature when he walks, trots, or canters. The gaits do usually remain pure when riding actively forwards, but when practising more complicated exercises in the school it is all too easy to spoil the rhythm and inhibit the horse's movements, causing him to step in an unnatural way. When schooling, purity of the gaits must be one of your first considerations.

One common example of an impure gait is the *disunited canter*. This is unmistakable because, being so different from the true

The disunited canter

The hindlegs are moving as for a right lead canter, but the forelegs are moving as for a left lead canter.

24

canter, it feels quite uncomfortable. If the horse is cantering to the right, for example, and leading with the right hindleg but leading in front with the left foreleg, he is said to be 'disunited in front'. He is 'disunited behind' if he leads with the correct foreleg but the incorrect hindleg. Being disunited is a sign that the horse is unbalanced. Probably the rider did not prepare him properly before striking off into canter.

Another example of an impure gait often occurs when a turn on the haunches is attempted. If the rider is unable to maintain the collection and the rhythm, the horse is liable to cease stepping with his inside hindleg, producing a faulty walk.

The walk is a gait which is particularly easy to spoil, and for this reason most of the horse's schooling should be done at trot and canter. Sometimes a horse will produce a hurried irregular walk, and in this case the gait can be improved by allowing him to work on a long rein, and encouraging him to relax. Another incorrect walk, which usually arises because of rider interference, is the *amble*. Here the horse moves his right hind and right fore legs together, followed by his left hind and left fore legs at the same time.

Faults at the trot include *forging*, where the horse's hindfoot strikes the shoe of his front foot, and *split diagonals*, where one foot of a diagonally opposite pair impacts with the ground before the other. These problems can be due to tiredness or loss of balance in the horse, or over-driving by the rider.

Lack of impulsion at canter can produce a faulty gait in which four footfalls can be detected, where the inside hindfoot impacts with the ground before the outside forefoot.

Forward riding

The horse has a natural inclination to move forwards, which is further enhanced by the rider's seat provided he sits correctly in the saddle. The mere fact that he has a weight to carry seems to inspire the horse to move. Do not tip forward or you will prevent this reaction, which is caused by the effect of gravity acting on your body, and you will have to exert your legs more than necessary to send the horse on.

Most riders either allow or encourage their horses to move too quickly. The speedy horse pushes himself horizontally forwards too much with his hindlegs, and this denies the rider the opportunity to influence the placement on the ground of the hind feet. It is then impossible to increase the weight-bearing capacity of the haunches, and the horse cannot learn to carry himself forwards in a graceful controlled fashion. Speed is one of the most common evasions practised by the horse, because it enables him to avoid the effort of carrying weight on his hind limbs.

Centuries ago, in the heyday of classical riding, when practising advanced school exercises, the masters found that unless their horses were allowed to gain a little ground at every step, they would become restive and refuse to move, or worse still run backwards. Hence they advised all riders to pay particular attention to making sure that their horses stepped forwards. For some reason this instruction has been interpreted differently in modern times and now everyone likes their horses to be onward bound as if they were out for a day's hunting.

There is no danger that by encouraging the horse to slow down in the riding school we will deprive him of his capacity for moving at speed. In fact it turns out that by slowing him down we can improve his facility for moving powerfully forwards in a controlled fashion at the extended gaits.

The horse must move eagerly without holding back, but he should do it *slowly*. Slowness is the key to developing the strength in the haunches that he needs if he is to bound forwards energetically.

The horse's deportment

The basic objectives of riding and schooling are impossible to achieve if the horse does not carry himself and his rider properly. His muscular development can only improve if he is unconstrained and free to move as nature intended. The aim is to teach him to carry himself better than he does when he looks at his best out in the paddock. Such a result will never be available if he is forced, by means of tension in the reins, to hold himself in some predetermined position, but experience shows that it will be achievable if he is trained to carry more weight on his haunches.

It is most important that your own deportment is impeccable, otherwise you will make life very difficult for your horse. If you cannot sit correctly and move in total harmony with him then he is likely to become tense or hollow his back, and no amount of school work will rectify the situation until your riding improves. The horse simply will be unable to move properly. Some horses that have been ridden badly in the past tense themselves up as a protection against any possible pain. In such cases, provided you can move as one with the horse, you should have no trouble in reducing the tension by schooling.

If the horse cannot swing his back freely he is likely to poke his nose out or lift his head up too high, supporting its weight on the lower neck muscles, which will bulge out in an ugly fashion. He will then be in a position from which he can very easily ignore your aids, and the whole riding experience will be totally unsatisfactory. The first schooling task for the horse who goes *above the bit* in this way is to encourage him to relax, by stroking his neck and yielding the reins. This will invite him to lower his head and stretch his topline. If you can see wrinkles in the horse's skin just in front of his withers, then his neck is not sufficiently relaxed, and you should encourage him to lengthen his frame a little more.

A harsh unyielding contact through the reins will always be detrimental to the horse's deportment. It may cause him to evade the discomfort by tucking his nose behind the vertical. This fault, which is known as being *behind the bit*, can be very difficult to correct, but until a correction has been effected all other schooling aims will have to be shelved, because without a proper contact it is not possible to engage the hindlegs, and this is the very essence of

Above the bit

Behind the bit

*Correct deportment
– on the bit*

schooling. To help this horse, drive him forwards strongly to encourage him to stretch his head forwards and down. Yield the reins whenever he makes an attempt.

A good check on the horse's deportment is to see if you can lower his head until the poll sinks down to the level of his withers. If he stretches slowly forwards and down seeking a contact with the bit then all is well. If not, then he is not yet basically correct. You must continue to work on his deportment until you can succeed with this test. You will be wasting your time if you pursue any other objectives while the horse is tense, resistant, or evading the aids.

If you are unsure whether the horse is moving correctly, or if you know he is not and you are unable to make an improvement, then seek the advice of a knowledgeable trainer.

Crooked horse on right rein

Straight horse on right rein

Straightness

In the same way that most people are either right handed or left handed, the vast majority of horses favour either the right or the left side of their bodies. You will no doubt recall seeing dogs running along with their tail ends held askew rather than directly behind their shoulders. Horses suffer from this design fault too! Success in keeping the horse straight depends on your ability to keep his shoulders directly in front of his haunches.

Most horses turn easily in one direction, but find it harder to turn the other way. At the same time the contact on the rein of the difficult side is usually too firm, whilst that on the other is so light that it is hard to achieve a good contact. The two sides of

the crooked horse are known as the *hollow side*, and the *stiff side*.

The root of the problem lies in the way the horse uses his hindquarters. Invariably there is an uneven loading of the hindlegs. When you ride the horse in greater collection you will be able to feel more easily any differences in the way he uses each of his hind limbs. One hindleg will seem strong but stiff, and the other will seem comparatively flexible but weak. Uneven use of the hind limbs limits the amount of collection that is obtainable, and because of this the potential for improving the horse by schooling is severely curtailed.

There is often some confusion when discussing crookedness. Some people consider that most horses are stiff to the left, whilst others find that the majority are stiff to the right! One would imagine that half the riders must be wrong, but in fact it transpires that different people have different ways of looking at the problem. When it is harder to turn to the left, the usual cause is stiffness in the horse's left hindleg, making him stiff to the left and hollow to the right. Some riders, however, cannot detect the uneven use of the hind limbs, and they attribute the problem to stiffness in the right side of the horse's body, which they believe is unable to stretch to the required length. In this case they consider the horse to be stiff to the right.

In order to get a good even lateral bend throughout the horse's body it is necessary that he takes sufficient weight on his inside hindleg. This is easier to achieve on the stiff side than it is on the hollow side where the hindleg is weaker. In some cases, difficulty in achieving the proper bend is really due to weakness in one hind limb, but some riders will attribute the problem to stiffness on that side, which adds to the confusion. Generally all riders feel the same things but interpret the signs differently.

We would like the horse to be as straight as possible so that we can canter just as easily on both leads, turn easily in either direction, and ultimately perform the canter pirouette both to the left and to the right. Crookedness mars everything we want to do with the horse, so it is well worthwhile trying to effect a cure.

No amount of schooling will ever make the horse perfectly ambidextrous, but it is certainly possible to make a good improvement. Some of the single track exercises will help a little, but marked improvements cannot be made without practising lateral exercises, so it is important to learn to ride these as soon as the horse is ready. *Shoulder-in* to the hollow side and *haunches-in* to the stiff side are particularly effective in correcting the uneven development of the hind limbs so that the horse becomes easier to straighten, but it is equally important to yield the rein on the stiff side so that the horse is not given the chance to lean on the bit.

Some riders work their horses more towards the stiff side than they do towards the hollow side, but this strategy is not particularly effective. The hollow side needs work too, because the hindleg on that side is weak and it will not get stronger unless it is made to engage and carry more weight.

3

EQUIPMENT

The saddle

A dressage saddle will be a sound investment if you intend to school your horse regularly. These saddles encourage a good riding position, and they allow the legs to lie close to the horse's sides. Compared to riding in a general purpose saddle, a dressage saddle feels more like riding bareback, except that it is more comfortable! It can be used for work over cavalletti, but it is not suitable for jumping larger obstacles.

If you have a general purpose saddle, then that should be perfectly adequate for schooling. On a young horse it will be superior to a dressage saddle, because it will be easier to stay on if the horse bucks. Unless you land back in exactly the right place on a dressage saddle you may well lose your balance and fall off.

Jumping saddles are not suitable for schooling because they prevent the legs from hanging down into the correct position for applying the aids.

The bridle

The snaffle

The snaffle is the correct bit to use for schooling. A jointed snaffle is preferable to an unjointed one, and a double jointed snaffle with a smooth central link or plate is perfectly acceptable if it proves a better fit. Contrary to popular belief the double jointed snaffle is milder than the single jointed variety.

A snaffle with cheeks can be useful, particularly if you have a young horse, or if your horse is not well trained. The reason is that many corrective measures involve yielding the contact on one rein. Under these circumstances, without the cheeks the bit is liable either to slide through the horse's mouth, or to put too much pressure against the side of his lips.

The upper cheeks of the snaffle can be fixed to the cheek pieces of the bridle using leather keepers. These help to keep the bit steady, and hold it in a position in which it contacts the bars more than the corners of the mouth, and this produces a more satisfactory result.

It is better to use a drop noseband than a cavesson when using this bit, because the upper cheeks of the bit might catch on a cavesson. The drop noseband should not be done up tightly. If the horse evades the bit by opening his mouth then the noseband can be made a little tighter for a few schooling sessions, but it is preferable to close the mouth with kind hands rather than tight leather straps.

The double bridle

Although it is appropriate to use the double bridle on a well trained horse, it is not suitable in the earlier stages of schooling, because it will restrict the horse's movement and inhibit the engagement of his hindlegs. It should never be used in an attempt to solve a schooling problem or to make the horse carry his head in some preferred position, and it must not be used as a brake. It is an instrument of precision to be used in producing a finer result on a well schooled animal.

Do not be tempted to use a double bridle too soon, or you will do more harm than good. If your horse does not go well in a snaffle then seek help with your schooling. The double bridle will not solve the problem.

There are no strict rules governing how the reins of a double bridle should be held. The traditional classical method is known as 'the three in one' because both curb reins and the left bridoon rein are held in the left hand, whilst the right hand holds the right bridoon rein. The left curb rein is held between the little finger and the third finger, the right curb rein between the third and second fingers, and the left bridoon rein is held outside the little finger. The free ends of the reins are all held together between the thumb and forefinger. The right bridoon rein is held between the little finger and the third finger of the right hand, the free end being fixed between the thumb and forefinger. When using this method the left hand is held centrally over the withers, whilst the right hand is held close beside it.

The main advantage of this method is that the horse always receives a consistent message from both sides of the curb. The reins can only be held this way when riding a very well trained horse. Strictly speaking, if it proves difficult to control a horse when holding the reins in the traditional manner then the horse is not yet ready to be ridden in a double bridle.

A more popular method of holding the reins is to take both left reins in the left hand and both right reins in the right hand. The bridoon reins are held outside and below the curb reins, either outside the little fingers or between the little and the third fingers. One or two fingers are used to separate the bridoon reins from the curb reins. The free ends are held between the thumbs and the first fingers.

In another less orthodox method both left reins are held in the left hand and both right reins in the right hand, but the two

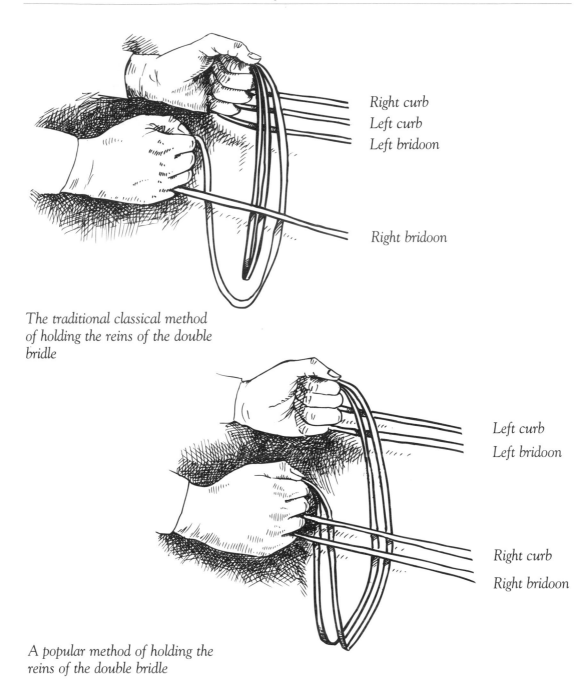

Right curb
Left curb
Left bridoon

Right bridoon

The traditional classical method of holding the reins of the double bridle

Left curb
Left bridoon

Right curb

Right bridoon

A popular method of holding the reins of the double bridle

reins in each hand are separated by the width of three fingers. The curb rein is held between the third and the little finger, whilst the bridoon rein is held between the thumb and the forefinger, together with the free end of the curb rein. The free end of the bridoon rein hangs down in the palm of the hand.

Spurs should always be worn when riding in a double bridle, in keeping with the principle that the driving aids should always exceed the stopping aids.

Other bits

Other bits such as Pelhams, Kimblewicks, or Dr Bristols are unsuitable for schooling. They are generally used in an attempt to provide a quick and easy solution to problems with the horse. They never have any beneficial effect in the long run, and they are no substitute for a properly organised schooling regime which will guarantee good and lasting improvements. Some of the more severe bits actually cause schooling problems, and they can set the training back a long way.

If you find that your horse seems to go better in a Pelham, for example, then what you are really doing is trying to compensate for your own lack of riding skill. You are placing constraints on his head and neck carriage to achieve a position that you prefer. Although you may feel more in control, you will not be influencing the demeanour of the horse's haunches in any beneficial way, and the long term prospects for his improvement by means of schooling will be severely diminished. The essence of the problem is that you control your horse too much through the reins. You need to learn how to control him through your seat and legs.

No matter what type of bit you normally use, when you ride in the manege you should change to a snaffle, and when you are convinced that you are in proper control you should use it all the time.

Auxiliary equipment

Martingales, draw reins, balancing reins, and so forth have no place in the riding school. They do not provide long term solutions, but work on the symptoms rather than the causes of problems and merely give a superficial impression of an improved condition.

The ability of a horseman can be judged by the simplicity of his equipment, and the truth is that a good rider needs nothing more than a saddle and bridle, and his own seat, legs, and hands to control a horse. This has been proved countless times over many hundreds of years, and is demonstrated today at the Spanish Riding School in Vienna where powerful stallions are managed without additional hardware.

From time to time new schooling aids come onto the market with the promise that they can produce good results quickly. If you have your horse's best interests at heart you would be well advised not to buy these, but to seek the help of a classically trained riding instructor instead.

Personal equipment

There are two items of personal equipment which you will find particularly useful when commencing work in the riding school: firstly a schooling whip, and secondly a pair of stout gloves. You may also wish to wear spurs, but these are by no means essential, and they are not particularly useful aids for schooling.

The schooling whip

A good length for the whip is 3' 3" or 3' 6", but a shorter one of 3' or slightly less will be more suitable if you are riding a pony. You will need to be able to use it in either hand, so if you are right handed, for example, and always carry a stick in that hand, then practise holding it in the left hand until that feels just as natural.

The whip should be used just behind your lower leg whenever an action from the latter produces no immediate response or an insufficient response. It is amazing how many riders are too accommodating with their horses. They put up with a lack of response and all sorts of insubordination without making any correction whatsoever, and they end up with horrible horses to ride as a result.

Obviously you should not use the whip if there is a good excuse for the horse not responding to your leg. It cannot help him to understand what he ought to do, and it cannot make it any easier for him to respond if he is hindered because he is holding himself in a poor posture. All it can do is to remind him to pay attention to your leg.

On a sensitive horse the whip can be applied by moving the hand outwards and pivoting the whip over the thigh until it comes to rest against the horse's side. On a thicker skinned animal a tap will be required. Do not hit the horse very hard with the schooling whip because being very thin in construction it will hurt him too much. The schooling whip is for aiding rather than for punishment. In the case of a young mischievous animal who needs to

be kept in order, a shorter thicker stick will be more suitable, as it will not hurt him when he is smacked, and it can be used on his shoulder quite effectively too.

In the riding school the current convention is to carry the whip in the inside hand, mainly because it will rub against the wall if you carry it on the outside. Another good reason for using it on the inside is that the horse's inside hindleg has to work harder through turns and on circles, and that is the leg you are more likely to want to assist. If the horse has a problem with one particular hindleg then you may choose to carry the whip on that side permanently. When you ride a complicated series of patterns and you are changing rein continually, you should not change the whip from side to side.

When you want to change the whip from one hand to the other, first take both reins into the whip hand, then turn that hand so that the thumb moves inwards and down and the whip moves outwards and up to an upright position. Turn the free hand inwards in a similar fashion and grasp the whip with the thumb down, close to the little finger of the whip hand. Let go with the other hand, and carry the whip across and down to its correct position. Finish by taking the reins back into two hands.

When using a double bridle and holding the reins in the 'three in one' manner, the whip is always held in the right hand. Traditionally the right hand was the sword hand, and the left the bridle hand

Sometimes difficulties arise which you will find easier to overcome if you carry two schooling whips. Some people imagine that this is cruel. One wonders if they would wear just one spur! The two whips are not intended as an extra battery of weapons for an errant horse. They are merely a convenience which will enable you to ride without continually having to change a single whip from side to side. This can be particularly useful when you start to teach the haunches-in, where one hindleg has to stay well engaged and the other has to move diagonally forwards and sideways.

Gloves

There are many times, particularly when riding horses that have not had the benefit of a proper basic education, when better results can be obtained by resting the hands down on the saddle to keep them steady. Without gloves the hands would soon become sore and blistered.

Leather gloves last much longer than other types, and they can also be used for lungeing, long reining, and for leading the horse in hand. Their only disadvantage is that they become slippery in wet weather, particularly when using plain leather reins; but that is not usually a serious problem within the confines of the manege.

Spurs

Spurs should be regarded as instruments of precision and not as a means of forcing the horse into subjection. Strictly speaking they are best reserved for advanced horses where there is some advantage to be gained from applying aids which are more refined and discrete. If the horse does not understand what to do when the legs are applied then he will not know what to do

when he feels the spurs either. This is why their usefulness is somewhat limited with the novice horse. Once he understands and responds correctly to the leg aids the spurs can be used to make the aids lighter. The horse can feel them more easily than the large expanse of the rider's boots.

Sometimes lazy horses react more to the spur than they do to the whip, and it is better to wear spurs if it enables you to ride without having to hit the horse all the time.

You must not wear spurs until you are in perfect control of your own legs. Be very careful that you do not use them accidentally. Keep your calves against the horse's sides when you aid with the spurs, and do not apply them too far back on the flanks, or you may provoke a buck.

Spurs must be blunt so they cannot hurt the horse. Even in the old days when long spurs with sharp rowels were the norm, knowledgeable horsemen were not so cruel as one might suppose. In the mid seventeenth century the Duke of Newcastle, a distinguished riding master, wrote that sharp spurs do much harm in the manege.

One might imagine that the longer the spurs the sharper their effects would be. This is not necessarily true, because it all depends on how they are used. Of course, on the heels of a maniac, or even a genuine rider unschooled in their use, long ones would do a lot of damage. An educated horseman, however, will be able to press the side of the shank of the longer spur against the horse's side, whereas with the short spur he would have no option but to nail him with the end.

Most riders attach their spurs at the level of the ankle. You will have more control over aiding with them, however, if you fix them lower down nearer the heel. With smaller horses and long-legged riders this will necessitate the use of longer spurs in order to reach their sides.

If you need spurs at all, perhaps the best advice would be to choose a pair with shanks measuring $3/4$" to $1^1/4$", and to fix them as low as possible whilst still being able to apply them easily.

4

MANEGE RIDING

Riding school protocol

There is no universally agreed code of behaviour in the riding school, and variations are not unknown. The protocol outlined below takes account of safety, whilst maximising the use of the manege, which is an expensive resource often in demand by many riders at the same time of the day:

- If you intend to loose school your horse, or if you wish to use cavalletti or jumps, then you must choose a time when others do not need the school, or when it can be specially reserved for such activities. If you wish to lunge or long rein, check with others already in the school before entering.

- Always announce your entry to riders who are already in the school: you might cause an accident if you enter unexpectedly. Similarly, ensure that others are made aware when you intend to leave.

- When in the manege do not deny entry to other riders except for reasons of safety. You do not need the arena all to yourself. Learn to work in company. Horses are gregarious by nature and often do not work so well alone.

- All riders have equal rights of access to the whole arena. Do not expect a newcomer to work in one half of the school just because you find it difficult to share the space. Never ask someone who is already in the manege to restrict themselves to a certain area on account of your arrival.

- If any rider meets with an accident, cease work immediately and do not continue until it is safe to do so.

- Be courteous to other riders and keep out of their way. When riding patterns, and when resting your horse at the walk, keep away from the walls so as to leave room for others to work on the perimeter track.

- You will not be able to complete every pattern that you commence. You will sometimes find other riders blocking your path, and you cannot expect them to move out of your way: you must turn away and repeat the pattern elsewhere when another opportunity arises.

- Anyone who causes a near collision should apologise. Experienced riders will be able to take avoiding action in good time, and they should take particular care not to obstruct novice riders who would be less well equipped to cope with the situation.

- Do not overtake other riders.

- When riding single-track patterns on the perimeter track and you meet another rider, also on a single track, coming towards you, then you have priority if you are on the left rein, but if you are on the right rein you must give way and move off the track. In other words, riders are expected to pass left hand to left hand.

- When riding with the forehand off the track at shoulder-in or haunches-out, or when riding counter-canter, you must give way to anyone working on a single track, regardless of which rein you are on. If you approach another rider who is also performing one of these exercises then whoever is on the left rein has right of way.

- If you approach a rider who is practising piaffe, passage, or haunches-in, then you must give way regardless of which rein you are on, because they always have right of way. The only exception to this

is if you are also practising one of these exercises, in which case whoever is on the left rein has priority.

Riding surfaces

Riding surfaces vary from manege to manege. The ideal surface for the horse to work on is good springy turf, where the foundation is firm and the grip is good. If you have the chance to work in a field and the going is suitable then make the most of the opportunity. Artificial surfaces are a poor substitute. It has even been suggested that they might be a contributory factor in the cause of some cases of obscure lameness in dressage horses.

If your horse is not used to working on a particular type of surface it will take a little time for him to adjust before he can move confidently. A deep surface provides an unnatural footing and he will find it hard work initially. The hardest time for the horse will be when you are teaching him something new. If you can do this on a surface he is comfortable on you will save a lot of time.

Schooling need not be restricted to sessions in the manege, it can also provide an interesting diversion while out hacking, and this will give you the chance to discover how the horse reacts to different surfaces.

The schooling session

The first phase of schooling should consist of limbering up. There are no hard and fast rules about how this should be done, but it is a good idea to start with a few minutes at the walk. It is important that the horse is properly toned up before the more vigorous exercises commence. He should be worked gradually, especially if he has been shut up in a stable for many hours beforehand. Individual horses vary in their requirements for limbering up. Some will benefit from working at the trot, and others will loosen up more quickly at the canter. As time goes by you will discover which is the best preparation for your horse.

While you are limbering up assess the basics: check that the horse moves freely forwards in a relaxed way without rushing, and stretches to seek a contact with the bit. If there are any problems in these areas then you must sort them out before progressing to more specific goals. Notice how straight the horse moves, and whether he works equally well in both directions. You will have to plan your schooling to take account of which side is stiff and which is hollow, so that in time any crookedness will diminish.

Proceed to work on the horse's specific schooling needs, which very likely you will have planned in advance. Either you will be hoping to work on and cure some problem, or you will be seeking to extend your horse's capabilities. Always have a good reason for every exercise you practise. Ride only movements that will be beneficial to the long term development of your horse.

Remember that there is plenty of space available in the school. Do not just ride around the edge all the time, or your work will be very boring. If there is a trench around the track because it has been used

many times since last it was levelled then keep away from it altogether.

Unless you have an advanced horse the trot will be the most important schooling gait. The walk is rather fragile and it is all too easy to spoil it. Reserve the walk for rest periods and for teaching new movements before you attempt them at trot or canter. Do not try to school the walk, or the chances are that you will destroy the gait. Any work you do at trot will have a generally beneficial effect on the horse and will improve his performance at walk and canter too.

The canter becomes increasingly more important as the horse's training progresses. On an advanced horse it is quite in order to start work at canter as soon as he has been limbered up. In nature the canter is used more than the trot, the latter being employed mainly as a short transitional phase between the walk and the canter.

Aim to make the work enjoyable so that the horse looks forward to his schooling sessions. Vary the patterns that you ride as much as possible, and repeat them all on both reins. Vary the gaits too: do not practise only a working trot or a working canter, but sometimes work in greater collection, and sometimes lengthen the stride. Alternate between exercises that encourage lateral bending, such as the circle, and those that promote longitudinal bending, such as lengthening and shortening strides.

Never modify the movement you are currently riding on account of one which is to follow. For example, a medium trot must always be the same regardless of whether it is to be followed by an extended trot or a halt.

It is a good idea to attempt something different every time you ride in the school. This will help to develop the mental capacities of your horse. You could start to teach him a new exercise, or you could practise a different combination of exercises or transitions.

Be sure the horse understands what you want him to do, and never make unreasonable demands. If he is resistant try to discover the reason why. Do not provoke him into resisting even more; he is far stronger than you, and you will lose the battle. You cannot expect schooling sessions to run smoothly if he has unhappy memories of earlier ones.

Normally you would expect to work in the school for some thirty to forty-five minutes; but on days when all goes well, finish early as a reward. Never stop when the horse has done something badly, or he will take it as a reward and try to oblige next time too! On days when you have particular difficulties you will need to stay in the school a little longer, but do not work the horse so hard that he becomes exhausted. Discontinue any approach that continually results in failure, or both you and your horse will get angry. Analyse the problem and develop an appropriate strategy. It is wise to practise something that is well within the horse's capabilities before you bring the session to a close.

The final phase of every schooling session should consist of relaxing and cooling the horse off at a free walk. You do not need to remain in the manege for this phase; you can ride out if you prefer.

5

IMPROVING YOUR RIDING ABILITY

Before you can hope to be effective in schooling your horse you must make certain that your position in the saddle and your riding skills are adequate. Your riding ability will depend largely on how well you sit. An ideal seat is one that enables the horse to move unhindered by his rider.

All the good riding academies of the past used to start their novice riders by working them every day on the lunge at a sitting trot without stirrups, for five or six months. This was followed by sessions on advanced school horses to learn to sit firstly the piaffe, and then the school jumps. By such methods riders developed a strong, effective, supple and well balanced seat.

Because the art of riding is now in decline, the latter part of this ideal training procedure is for all practical purposes no longer possible. The lungeing phase, however, still has everything to commend it: there really is no better way to develop a good seat. If you have the opportunity to learn on the lunge then take advantage of

it, as it is the quickest way to acquire the foundation that you need if you are to become a successful rider.

It is by no means essential for the beginner to learn on the lunge, but those who are unable to do so will have a much harder task ahead, because they will be expected to learn to control the horse at the same time as learning how to sit. The process will then take much longer, and the riders will need a great deal of self-discipline if they hope to rise above mediocrity.

Posture

Unmounted practice

A good approximation to the correct riding posture can be obtained by standing with your back to a wall. Place your feet about two feet apart with the heels a couple of inches away from the wall, and point your toes directly forwards. Bend

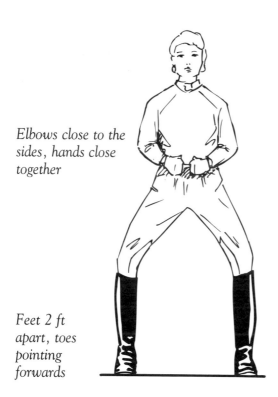

Elbows close to the sides, hands close together

Feet 2 ft apart, toes pointing forwards

Head touching the wall

Shoulders touching the wall

Small of back an inch from the wall

Base of spine touching the wall

Knees vertically above toes

Heels 2 inches from the wall

your knees until they are vertically above your toes.

Hold the base of your spine and the back of your head against the wall. Flatten your shoulder blades and hold the top of your shoulders against the wall. Move your hips back and flatten the lumbar spine until the small of your back is about an inch away from the wall.

Allow your upper arms to hang down vertically and hold your elbows close to your hips. Lift your forearms until they lie just below the horizontal. Hold your wrists straight and keep your fists clenched lightly with the thumbs uppermost and the knuckles almost touching.

The Three-point seat

When mounted in the saddle your body should be balanced above your seat, which should be placed centrally in the deepest part of the saddle. Because the seat forms the basis of the whole aiding system, it is important to perfect it.

Throughout the last two hundred years the classical seat has remained virtually unchanged, and has sometimes been described as a 'three-point seat'. In this terminology the stability and firmness of the pelvis, which enables it to move in unison with the horse's back, is considered to derive from its connection with the saddle in three prime regions: the two seat bones and the crotch. Because of the bony nature of the seat, you will easily feel your two seat bones contacting the saddle. You should also be aware of the support provided by the fleshy area between and to the front of the seat bones. Regardless of what you are doing with your horse the positions of these three areas in the saddle never change; but the distribution of your body weight over them may vary.

Do not round your back, or you will move your crotch away from the saddle and you will be liable to rock to and fro on the seat bones. Not only would such a seat provide an unstable and ineffective basis for control, but it would also be liable to harm the horse's back. You must also take care too not to go to the opposite extreme and hollow your back, as that would lighten the weight on the seat bones and put too much weight on the fork. With a hollow back your upper body would be effectively disconnected from your seat, and aiding through the seat would then be impossible.

Unless you are deliberately aiding by changing your weight distribution over the three points of the seat, your pelvis must not move relative to the horse's back, but should move as one with the horse as though it were a part of him. Your lower back must provide a mobile, resilient connection between your pelvis and your upper body, by moving in such a way that the latter appears to be upright and motionless as the horse moves along. It is the lower back that must absorb the energy of the movement in the horse's back. If it were immobile or stiff, the energy would be transmitted to your upper body, and the resulting uncontrolled movement of your torso would disturb your seat, give you and your horse a bumpy ride, and destroy the effectiveness of your aids.

If you have a well trained horse who collects himself naturally then you will be able to relax your lower back a little more than if you have a novice horse to ride. With the novice you will need to flatten your lower back more often and allow your body weight to act more through your seat bones, to encourage the horse to engage his hindlegs and carry you properly on a braced back.

Leaning forwards or backwards

Do not allow your shoulders to move in front of your hips or the effectiveness of your seat will be lost and the influence of your weight will no longer encourage the horse to move forwards. It is also important that you keep your head in its proper position. You may feel the need to look down at your horse to see how well or how badly he is going. If you do this do not move your head, but look down your nose instead.

You will rarely if ever need to lean forwards when schooling. You may, however, need to lean backwards in some circumstances. Leaning behind the vertical provides a safety seat in emergency situations. If the horse bucks, for example, you will not fall off provided you lean back in good time. The rider who tilts forwards is always vulnerable. On a difficult horse, angle your pelvis back a little, so that if he does anything that might cause you to lose your balance you are ready to lean back without delay, and you will find your chances of avoiding an accident are greatly improved.

You will also find that you can apply more powerful driving and stopping aids with your seat when you lean behind the vertical. You will not need to do this once you have mastered the aids and your horse is responding correctly, but as a temporary measure you will find it is of invaluable assistance. It will be particularly helpful when you are learning to ride direct downward transitions. It is the act of leaning back that is effective, rather than actually being behind the vertical, so you should return to the upright position after you have applied the aid.

Once you have developed an effective seat and you have well schooled horses to ride you will be able to remain upright virtually all the time, but if you try to achieve everything from this ideal postural position before you have become an effective rider, you will probably never discover how you can influence the horse through your seat.

Aiding with the legs

Do not allow your thighs or the stirrups to support any of your weight, or you will not be able to use your legs freely when you apply the aids, and furthermore your ability to apply weight aids through the seat will be severely diminished. It is important to discipline yourself not to gain any assistance from the stirrups. This applies even when you rise to the trot. Imagine that you have an egg between each foot and the stirrup iron, and never apply enough pressure to break it.

Kicking with the heels is both ineffective as an aid and ugly to observe. Use the insides of your calves instead, and direct

the pressure inwards and slightly forwards. Keep your legs in contact with the horse's sides all the time so that he can sense changes in pressure and not be surprised by a sudden contact.

The light seat

So long as the application of your body weight is constant, it will be of no inconvenience whatsoever to the horse; but if you cannot conform to his movements with your lower back then he will tend to bump you out of the saddle, at which time, to him, you will feel lighter, until you fall down into the saddle again, at which point you will seem much heavier. This will make locomotion very tiresome for the horse, and will be detrimental to his development, particularly if he is a young horse whose back is not yet very strong.

It is not possible to sit heavily or lightly in a controlled manner. The laws of nature do not permit you to change your mass while you are riding: regardless of how you sit, the horse always has exactly the same burden to carry. You will hear instructors talking about a light seat in which you put more weight into the stirrups and onto your crotch, at the same time lightening the pressure of your seat bones in the saddle. This description is a misnomer; it is not a light seat at all. It merely changes the distribution of your weight so that your centre of gravity shifts forwards a few inches. The main advantage to the horse is that your body will not bounce on his back, and he is guaranteed a smooth ride.

When using the light seat, your opportunities for schooling the horse are severely curtailed, because you are not in a position to influence his back or hindquarters. By all means use the light seat when limbering up or while out hacking, but if your horse has a weak back and cannot accept the full seat for any length of time, then shorten the schooling sessions and work him gradually until he becomes stronger, but adopt the classical seat.

Feeling the movement

You must develop a feel for how the horse is moving from the sensations that you perceive through his back. In the early stages of learning to ride you should glance down at the shoulders or legs and try to associate their position and movement with the motion of your seat.

You will find that each side of the horse's back rises slightly as the hind foot on that side presses backwards against the ground. At the same time the other side sinks slightly. You will need to accommodate this slight undulating motion in your hips, but be careful to allow it to happen naturally. Do not deliberately exaggerate the movement.

Exercises on horseback

In the first phase of schooling, while you are limbering up your horse, it is a good idea to take the opportunity to do a few exercises to improve your posture and loosen yourself up. This will be particularly worthwhile if you are stiff after your normal daily routine.

Always be safety conscious when practising exercises on horseback. Never attempt anything that does not seem safe under the prevailing conditions. Stop immediately if you begin to lose your balance, and do not continue until your seat is perfectly secure again.

The exercises suggested below should be practised at the walk unless stated otherwise:

- 'Walk' yourself down into the saddle by moving one thigh back and the other forwards, and vice versa. Repeat several times and finish by taking both thighs back, placing them flat against the saddle flaps.

- Twist your body left and right at the waist several times, and then straighten up.

- Keeping your head up and your back flat, circle your shoulders by taking them forwards, hunch them up, move them backwards and then down. Repeat the exercise a few times and finish by holding them back and down in the correct position with the shoulder blades flat.

- Keeping your knees and thighs in place circle your lower legs by moving them away from the horse's sides, then backwards, and finally slide them forwards against the horse's coat back into place.

- It is very important that you are able to use your legs independently. You must be able to use one without moving the other, and you must be able to apply one in a different position and with a different intensity to the other. Practise holding one leg still while you circle the other lower leg. This exercise you should try at walk, trot, and canter. When you practise it at the trot try both the sitting trot and the rising trot, both with and without stirrups.

- Loosen your ankles by circling the feet. Without moving your thighs, knees, or lower legs, lift your toes up, turn them out, press them down, and then move them in again and raise them to their proper position.

- To improve your balance in the saddle try variations of the rising trot where you sit for two beats and rise for one, or sit for one and rise for two. You can try these with or without stirrups, or with one stirrup only.

- An adhesive seat at trot is one of the primary requirements of good riding. To develop a more adhesive seat, practise leaning back in the saddle at trot at various angles up to about forty five degrees. When you lean back, do so by rocking back on the two seat bones, thereby lightening the pressure on the crotch. Your back must remain straight. As you lean forwards again to approach the upright position try to obtain the smoothest sitting trot you can. Adjust the motion of your lower back until you achieve the best result.

If you hold on to the pommel of the saddle and pull yourself down firmly, the feeling this produces in your seat will be the one you should aim to obtain when you are not holding on.

- One valuable exercise at canter is to turn your body from side to side in the rhythm of the movement. Do not turn at the waist but move your inside hip forward too, pressing your inside seat bone forward into the saddle. The whole inside of your body should move as a unit, and the resulting drive from your inside shoulder and seat should be synchronised with the push from the horse's hindlegs as they propel him forwards. Your inside shoulder should swing back quickly during the period of suspension ready to start the next forward swing when the outside hindleg strikes the ground again.

Try this exercise on both canter leads. It is an important exercise because it demonstrates, albeit in a very exaggerated way, the correct motion of your body at canter. It will counteract any tendency you may have to swing backwards and forwards. The feeling at canter should always be one of pushing the inside of your seat forwards at every stride. It is not normally necessary to swing your shoulders too, but you can do so if you need to give a more powerful driving aid.

- Ultimately you will get better results from your horse when you can ride with your legs stretched well down, but it takes time to achieve this ideal position. Riding without stirrups from time to time will help you to develop a better seat in the long term, and eventually you will be able to ride with longer stirrups. There is nothing to be gained by riding with the stirrups too long. Your legs will not remain in contact with the horse's sides, and you will be continually groping for the irons.

The rising trot

If your sitting trot is not perfect then the horse will find your rising trot more comfortable. When rising to the trot in the manege you should allow the motion of the horse to push you just out of the saddle, rather than deliberately trying to stand up in the stirrups. Your seat should only just leave the saddle, your body should remain upright, and you should sit back down gently. Practise the rising trot without stirrups, and then when you take them back, rise in exactly the same way, without supporting any weight on the irons.

When you ride a collected trot you should always remain sitting. This trot should be sufficiently comfortable to sit to anyway, and rising to it would look rather peculiar.

If you are rising to the trot on a circular track then you should sit in the saddle when the horse's outside forefoot and inside hindfoot are on the ground, and be out of the saddle when the inside fore and outside hind are on the ground. This will give you more control of the inside hindleg than if you sit down when the inside diagonal is on the ground.

Riding turns and circles

When progressing along curved lines the horse should be bent towards the direction in which he is turning, and remain upright rather than leaning into the turn.

Some instructors will tell you that the horse's spine should be bent around the curve along which he is ridden. It is now known that this is not possible. With the exception of the neck and tail the spine is too rigid to bend to such an extent.

When moving on curved lines the horse must not lean into the turn...

...but must remain upright.

Nevertheless the whole body of the horse should have the appearance of being so bent. This is achieved by the horse bending his neck, turning his shoulders, engaging his inside hindleg, and lowering his inside hip.

Remaining upright is æsthetically pleasing to the eye, and enables you to change the bend or the pattern you are riding without first having to make a vertical adjustment to the horse's position. The horse will not be able to remain upright and bent in the required direction if he carries too little weight on his inside hindleg. Correctly ridden turns and circles help to strengthen the hindquarters because they oblige the inside hindleg to participate in weight support.

In order to help the horse to turn you should turn your upper body in the required direction so that your outside shoulder moves forwards and your shoulders remain parallel to those of the horse as he makes the turn. Do not lean over sideways. At the same time, keeping your inside leg in place, slide back your outside knee, thigh, and lower leg, until your heel has moved back about four inches. This postural change should cause your weight to shift slightly towards the inside of your seat. The whole effect will encourage the horse to bend and turn in the required direction.

The more advanced animal will be able to negotiate tighter turns and smaller circles than the novice. The latter will not be able to bend his inside hindleg or lower his inside hip to the same extent, and he may need some extra guidance from the reins. If he is very green you can use an *opening rein*

or *leading rein* to lead him into the turn with the inside rein: turning your hand outwards slightly so that the thumb leads the way, take your inside forearm out sideways away from your body, without losing the contact with the bit. Yield the outside rein to allow the horse to turn.

Some care should be exercised when changing the bend from left to right or vice versa. Always change the bend in good time so that the tip of the horse's nose follows exactly the pattern you are

The 'opening' or 'leading' rein can be a useful aid when turning a green horse.

The left forearm is taken out sideways to turn the horse to the left.

attempting to ride. If you change the bend too late you will have to make an ugly correction by moving the horse's head suddenly from one side to the other. Adjust your seat and the position of your legs, making good use of your new inside leg to

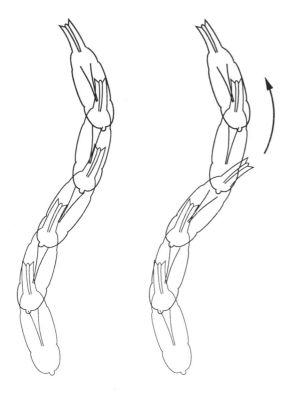

(Left) Correct change of bend. (Right) Late change of bend – the tip of the horse's nose does not descibe the intended pattern.

ensure that the horse remains upright and carries enough weight on his new inside hindleg.

It is chiefly your seat and legs which should be responsible for bending and turning the horse. In former times when horses were trained for the battlefield, the riders had only one hand free for the reins, and they quickly learned to ride with their seat and legs. The modern rider has both hands available, and is inclined to rely on them too much. To check that you are aiding correctly, and not cheating with the reins, you should practise riding turns, circles, and changes of bend and direction whilst holding the reins in one hand. You are

strongly advised to persevere with this until you succeed.

Feedback

When trying to improve your riding, react to all the sources of feedback that you have available. The positions of your hands, arms, feet, and legs can be checked by visual inspection. Make adjustments if faults show up in photographs or videos. Make use of mirrors whenever they are available. Shadows too can give very useful clues about your posture and motion in the saddle.

Always act on comments from observers. Riding lessons can be useful here, but it is important to select a knowledgeable teacher. Someone who is able to train horses will be able to advise on schooling your horse in addition to perfecting your equitation.

One word of warning here is that not all instructors are committed to the principles of classical riding: in other words they may not have in mind the objectives that you have selected as your goals. Many older British instructors were neither trained nor examined by anyone with a classical background. Fortunately a number of classical masters now visit Britain on a regular basis, and many of the younger teachers are better informed than their predecessors.

Broadening your knowledge

Take every opportunity you can to observe other riders. Attend lectures, demonstrations and public training sessions whenever possible. These can be wonderful sources of inspiration, and they can also give you the chance to learn from other people's mistakes. Read as many books as you can.

Riding and schooling cannot successfully be studied in isolation. You would be well advised to gain a rudimentary knowledge of related equestrian topics. Although you do not need to study them in depth, you ought to take an interest in farriery, saddlery, first-aid and veterinary matters, feeding, and stable management. Some knowledge of anatomy will help you to appreciate how the horse moves, for example, but learning the names of the various bones and muscles will not help you to ride, any more than knowing the chemical composition of paints would help an artist to produce a masterpiece.

The better you understand everything that has an impact on the life of your horse, the more you will understand his mentality. You will feel more empathy for him, and this in turn will have a beneficial effect on your riding. As an added bonus you will be able to verify that those to whom you entrust the care of your horse carry out their duties in a satisfactory manner.

6.

CONTACT

Contact is the term used to describe the connection between the horse's mouth and the rider's hands. Under ideal conditions there should be no tension between mouth and hand, and neither party should feel any more than the weight of the reins.

The bit is a passive aid whose prime function is to provide a fixed reference point defining the limit to which the horse is able to stretch his topline. Without this limiting factor the horse would be able to lengthen his frame and evade our attempts at engaging his hindlegs. A secondary function of the bit is to assist, in collaboration with the seat and legs, the lateral bending and turning of the horse.

It is the horse, not the rider, who must contact the bit. Whenever the reins are lengthened, the horse must stretch his nose gradually forwards and down to seek a contact with the bit again. If he were to hold his head back and not try to find a

contact, it would be pointless to shorten up the reins just for the sake of closing the gap: neither the reins nor the horse's topline would be participating in the aiding system. You can encourage the horse to stretch by stroking his neck, which will help him to relax, and you can choose patterns and exercises that will promote engagement of the hindlegs so that he will begin to use his back correctly.

If your reins have become so long that the horse cannot stretch far enough to take up the slack, then you should shorten them so that he is able to establish a contact. If you wish to collect the horse then you must use your seat and legs to engage his hindquarters, and simultaneously take up the slack occasioned by his modified posture. Do not try to collect him by shortening the reins alone.

Many books on riding explain the effects of different types of bit. The snaffle is supposed to raise the horse's head, and the claim for the curb is that it makes

If the horse holds his head up and will not contact the bit…

…do not shorten up the reins to establish a contact…

…but stroke the horse's neck and encourage him to relax until he stretches forwards.

him flex at the poll. One wonders if the authors of these books had a proper understanding of the sort of contact required in classical riding, because although it is possible to cause these effects by applying pressure to the horse's mouth, in practice such activities are counter-productive. Setting the position of the head and neck by means of the reins does not further the horse's physical development in any constructive way. On the contrary, it destroys the relaxation and interferes with the freedom of movement, which are quintessential ingredients of good riding.

It is not really appropriate to discuss the action of a bit, because within the civilised confines of the riding school the bit should not be used in an active way at all. Because it is widely assumed that horse riding does involve an active use of the reins, it is generally believed that the long-cheeked curbs that were used in bygone days were particularly cruel and forceful. In the hands of the average modern rider there would certainly be cause for concern, but in general the old masters of classical riding knew how to use their equipment with delicacy and precision, and they did not pull on the reins. In the wrong hands, or with incorrectly trained horses, such equipment would obviously do appalling damage, and in fact horse's jaws have been broken by their riders pulling hard on powerful curbs. In such cases, of course, it was the riders who were cruel and forceful; there was nothing intrinsically wrong with the curbs themselves.

Situations do arise from time to time when an active use of the reins is unavoidable, but these fall outside the scope of academic riding. You are allowed to use the reins, for example, to prevent the horse from eating the hedgerow, or to replace his head in the correct position if he has been looking around and not concentrating, but you must release the tension straight away so as not to imprison his head with the reins.

Steadying the reins

The only correct position for the horse's head is one which is in balance with the rest of his body. It is usually correct when he is free in the paddock, where there is nothing to interfere with the way he chooses to carry himself. In order that the head can adopt the proper position it must be given freedom, not constraint. If the horse carries his head badly it is a sign that there is a problem with his overall deportment. Using the reins and bits to force his head into a better position would not effect a postural correction, but would only lead to the various parts of his anatomy being out of balance with one another.

The horse's head carriage will often be at its best when you lunge him in side-reins. These provide just the sort of stability that he requires when he seeks a contact with the bit. He must find something positive, consistent, and totally passive. If you can provide a contact with just these qualities when you are holding the reins then your horse will display a good head carriage under the saddle too.

Side-reins provide a stability that enables the horse to display a good head carriage.

An adhesive seat and steady elbows will give a side-rein like stability, and allow the horse to adopt a correct posture.

In order for the aiding system to work properly the reins must effectively connect the bit to your seat, so that the rein and seat aids operate exactly in unison and give one consistent message to the horse. It is perhaps unfortunate that the reins cannot be attached directly to your hips instead of having to act through the intermediaries of your hands, wrists, forearms, elbows, upper arms, shoulders, and torso. In order to ensure that a proper connection is supplied via this somewhat circuitous route it is useful to stabilise your elbows against your sides.

Most instructors expect their pupils to carry their hands some four inches above the horse's withers. Indeed, this is the correct position to adopt if you are an experienced rider and you are riding an advanced horse. In other circumstances it is generally easier to provide the sort of contact that the horse requires if you rest one or both of your hands on the pommel of the saddle. Since it is rare to have the pleasure of riding a well trained horse, the usual situation is that it is necessary to stabilise the reins in this way.

It is particularly important that you do not allow your arms to move about whenever the horse moves his head. This is one of the most common mistakes made in riding. Your arms must be held as though they were part of your upper body. To follow all the actions of the horse's head and neck with the arms would serve no functional purpose whatsoever; there would be no point in having reins at all.

Some instructors will tell you that the horse moves his head backwards and forwards at walk and at canter, and will insist that you follow this movement with your arms. When the horse does move in this way it is a sign that he has not been trained correctly. He does not engage his hindlegs properly or swing his back. He is not on the aids, and he is unbalanced. If you continue to conform to faulty movements such as these whenever they are offered by your horse then you will never succeed in improving him through schooling.

Yielding, and passive resistance

The most important of all the aids that can be administered via the reins is yielding the pressure. This is the only way to produce a horse that is light in the hand.

Whenever you have the opportunity, try to lighten the contact and see for how long the horse continues to move correctly. Being able to detect all the moments when the rein pressure can be relaxed is an important riding skill which you must do your best to acquire.

Passive resistance is applied through the reins by holding them steady in place and not yielding. It is accompanied by a stillness in the seat, effected by holding firm the muscles of the abdomen. A backward pull on the reins is never allowed. It is at times of passive resistance that the fixed reference point is provided to prevent the horse lengthening to evade the engaging effect of the seat and legs. Passive resistance must always be followed by yielding.

Yielding can be used as a means of relaxing the horse and encouraging him to stretch his topline. It should not be administered as a sudden slackening of both reins, but should be done alternately on each rein in time with the horse's movement, so that a contact is always maintained on one rein. The pressure on each rein should be released, without letting it hang loose, at the same time as the horse's shoulder on the same side advances, and it should be accomplished by means of a small movement in the whole upper body, rather than by moving the arm forwards. The effect should be an imperceptible 'breathing' from side to side of the upper body in the rhythm of the horse's movement. A pleasing appearance of stillness in the rider is caused by moving in harmony with the horse in this way. The rider who tries to remain motionless will move in opposition to his horse.

Turns and circles

A basic method of turning

When the horse is relaxed and moving properly he will seek a contact with the bit in the usual way. If you lengthen the reins he will stretch a little more and lengthen his frame until he finds the bit again.

If instead of yielding both reins you yield just one of them, say the left one, his instinctive reaction will be to turn his head and neck to the right in an attempt to reestablish a contact on left side of his mouth. In doing so he will change direction and make a turn to the right. Your horse will then be 'on the right rein': he will be turning towards the right because of the contact on the right rein.

Although the yielding outside rein will assist the horse to turn, it will not be sufficient in itself to produce a good bend. You will also need to apply the usual leg and seat aids for turning: take your outside leg back and turn your upper body towards the direction of the bend. This is the most basic way of riding turns and circles. It is very important that all riding horses, novice and advanced alike, should be able to negotiate turns in this manner. If it does not work then there is a very fundamental problem with the horse's training. Either he is not relaxed, or he is not seeking a contact with the bit as he should.

Having succeeded in yielding the left rein to make a right turn, you can straighten the horse up again by yielding the right rein, turning your upper body back to face the front again, and taking your left leg

The rider maintains the contact on the right rein and yields the left to help the horse to turn right.

The horse is on the right rein.

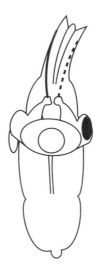

If, assisted by the right leg of the rider, the horse can support himself on his right hindleg, a good right turn can be obtained by maintaining the contact on the left rein and yielding the right.

The horse is between the inside leg and the outside rein.

forwards into position by the girth. Yield the right rein a little more and you will be ready to start a turn to the left. Practise making several changes of direction using this method, always yielding the new outside rein to help the horse to turn. He will remain unconstrained, free in his action, relaxed, and in a pleasantly rounded frame.

If you experience any difficulty in producing good turns you may find it helps if you steady your inside hand by resting it on the saddle. To help the horse to relax, stroke the outside of his neck with your outside fist and then bring it back into the normal position again.

An advanced method of turning

If you wish to collect the horse when riding turns, as you certainly will if your horse is anything but a novice, then you will soon discover that there is a disadvantage in turning by yielding the outside rein. When you use your seat and legs to collect the

horse you will not be able to engage his hindlegs without the contact on the outside rein. He will evade your influence, either by turning his head inwards or by moving his hindquarters over towards the outside.

After bending the horse in the required direction using the normal positioning aids and yielding the outside rein, reestablish the contact on the outside rein and yield instead the inside rein, and you will find that you can collect the horse more easily. Be sure to keep your inside leg on the girth to help him to engage his inside hindleg so that it gives adequate support for his weight.

You should find that you are able to keep the horse bent in spite of yielding the inside rein, and that he will not try to turn his head the other way to seek a contact with the bit. If he does turn his head and start to move away in the other direction then you will have to continue turning him largely under the influence of the inside rein, and you will have to keep him in a longer frame for a while until his hindlegs become stronger and he is able to bend the inner one sufficiently to hold himself in balance in the curved position.

If you are successful in keeping your horse bent whilst lightening the inner rein then you will find that collection becomes even easier to obtain because the engagement of the inside hindleg is no longer hindered by pressure on the rein. You will have succeeded in riding the horse 'between the inside leg and the outside rein'.

To see if your horse is ready for this advanced method of turning there is a useful test you can try. Let the inside rein hang loose, and then lengthen the outside rein gradually. He must remain bent to the inside and must stretch forward and down to find a contact on the outer rein. You will find this is harder when you are turning towards the horse's stiff side. If he fails the test then he is not yet ready to be turned by this advanced method, and you should continue to use the more basic method.

Riding between the inside leg and the outside rein is an advanced concept that cannot successfully be applied to novice horses. Many riders try to hold their horses on the outside rein long before they are ready. When it is done too soon the horse ceases to move in a relaxed frame, and it is the rider who establishes the contact with the bit rather than the horse, which is totally wrong. The contact on the outside rein is usually too strong, and the net result

is a horse that is tense and cannot lengthen his frame.

You will sometimes hear instructors calling for 'more outside rein' through corners or on circles. They have misunderstood the concept of riding between the inside leg and the outside hand. They forget that riding is supposed to be all about lightness, relaxation and balance. Of course you will need to shorten the reins if they get too long, but as a general rule in riding you never need 'more rein'.

The crooked horse

No horse is perfectly straight in his action, and this further complicates the issue of contact. Hitherto we have assumed a straight horse; but most horses will tend to take a relatively strong contact on one side and a light contact on the other. The objective is to teach the horse to take an equal contact on both sides of his mouth, and to this end it is important to yield more with the rein on the stiff side so that he is obliged to contact his less favourite side.

When circling towards the hollow side it is better to use the basic method of turning, keeping a contact on the lighter inner rein and yielding the outer rein, to discourage the horse from leaning on the bit on the stiff outer side. When circling towards the stiff side it is quite in order to try to ride with a contact on the outer rein because that is the side the horse prefers not to contact.

7

SIMPLE TRANSITIONS

Downward transitions

These include changes from extension to collection in addition to changes from canter to trot, trot to walk, and walk to halt. It is also possible to change from extension to collection at the same time as changing the gait, so one could, for example, change directly from an extended trot to a collected walk.

There is some similarity in the way the rider should assist the horse to bring about all the downward transitions. The aids can best be understood by considering first the halt.

The halt

The horse can come to rest in a variety of ways. The worst case is the type of abrupt stop he uses when he refuses to jump an obstacle. He sticks his front limbs forwards to use them as a brake, which arrests his forward movement so quickly that the rider is liable to fall off. At the other end of

the scale it is possible for the horse to halt with deeply lowered haunches, possibly even lifting his front feet off the ground. In the past these halts 'on the haunches' were commonplace in the riding school. Although neither of these extremes is desirable, some degree of lowering of the haunches will help to produce a smooth, comfortable, well controlled stop, and for this reason it is important the horse is trained to take the weight back towards the hindquarters when coming to rest.

For the rider, the ability to ride good downward transitions is an extremely important accomplishment. A necessary prerequisite is to have a good seat which can conform to the motion of the horse's back at all paces. Bringing the horse to a standstill can be considered as a two-part problem: firstly he must be brought more onto his haunches, and secondly his forward movement must be arrested.

There are aids which can be applied to help the horse to shift his weight to the rear and lower his haunches, but in the early stages of his training these aids will not be very effective. The horse's ability to bend the joints of his hindlegs is something that develops gradually as a result of systematic schooling. In practice it will be difficult to accomplish good smooth halts before he has mastered the various lateral movements, because he will not be able to bend his joints sufficiently until he has been exercised in this way.

The aids for lowering the haunches involve redistributing your body weight so that it acts more through the seat bones. Keeping your hips as the pivotal point, move the lower part of your pelvis slightly forwards so that the small of your back becomes flatter, and your seat bones press a little more firmly into the saddle. Maintain a passive resistance with the reins while you do this, and hold the horse with your thighs, otherwise the movement of your pelvis will merely cause your upper body to move further back and it will exert no influence on the horse. The connection via the reins and your thighs keeps your body properly fixed to that of the horse so that the action of your seat can be transmitted to his haunches. Use your legs as necessary to keep the horse's hindlegs well engaged.

Although the ultimate aim is to sit upright while halting, a good exercise to practise in the early stages is to lean back in the saddle while you apply the aids. Your upper body will then act as a lever which increases the effect of the movement in your pelvis, and you will quickly learn to develop a seat which is effective in its stopping ability.

The aids for arresting the forward movement should be applied synchronously with those for lowering the haunches: the two components of the halting process complement each other. Hold your knees and thighs firmly against the saddle and tighten your abdominal muscles. The idea of this is to damp down the motion of your seat, which has hitherto been conforming to the motion of the horse's back. This will impede the horse's locomotion and shortly bring him to a standstill.

As the horse becomes more experienced and his balance improves you will not need to depend so much on the passive resistance with the reins when halting. It should be possible to stop a correctly schooled horse on loose reins just by stopping the movement of your own body.

Other methods of stopping the horse, such as tightening the reins or using more powerful bits, would interfere with the engagement of his hindlegs. This would prevent him from lowering his haunches and would cause him to stop on the forehand. Such transitions usually require a lot of force from the rider, are unpleasant to ride and do nothing to further the horse's training.

Rough and ready techniques should be reserved for emergency situations. They should play no part in civilised riding. If you find that horse riding helps to develop your arm muscles then you are not riding correctly. It is your abdominal muscles and thighs that should become stronger.

The half-halt

The half-halt is the first part of the halting process. It consists of shifting the horse's weight more onto his haunches and getting him to the stage where he has almost but not quite come to rest. At this stage one could complete the halt, or one could ask the horse to move on again.

The horse should always move in such a way that he remains under control and can be stopped easily. With most horses their balance gradually deteriorates, and they gain some advantage over their riders, who thus begin to lose control. The half-halt is a useful means of restoring the status quo. There is nothing wrong in using the full halt to bring the horse back under control but this would be more time-consuming and would disrupt the flow, so it is usually more convenient to ride the half-halt.

At any one time, no more than three more strides of the current gait should be required before you can effect any downward transition. If you need more than three strides then your horse is out of control and you are merely a helpless passenger. You should try to keep the horse going all the time in the way that he moves immediately prior to these last three strides. Use the half-halt as often as necessary to keep him properly under control, and to increase his responsiveness to the aids for downward transitions.

Another use of the half-halt is in lightening the rein contact. It is always easy to achieve a light contact when you ride in an uncollected way on long reins, but when you ride in collection, although you need much shorter reins, you should not put any more pressure on the horse's mouth. Whenever the horse starts to take a stronger contact, ride a half-halt to rebalance him and then yield the pressure on the reins again. In time you will have a very good horse that can always be ridden on the lightest of reins.

Trot to walk

This is one of the easiest downward transitions for both horse and rider. It should be effected by applying a half-halt and restricting the motion of your pelvis so that the horse is unable to continue in trot. If you have been rising to the trot, change to the sitting trot before you ask for the walk.

Aim to produce a smooth transition. The horse must change directly from a pure trot to a pure walk without any hesitation. Having arrived at the walk, keep him active. He must not assume that he is allowed a rest period.

Canter to trot

The restricting influence of your seat applied via a half-halt should be largely responsible for bringing about this transition. In order to proceed at canter the horse depends on your seat conforming to the motion of his back, so if you cease the cantering motion of your own body the horse will stop cantering too. On a sensitive horse all you should need to do is to square up your shoulders by taking the outer one back to the level of the inner one, and sit still.

If you find that you cannot sit to the trot that follows the canter then you would be well advised to spend more time practising the sitting trot, because you will not succeed in schooling your horse until you have mastered it.

Extension to collection

As with the transitions down from one gait to another, downward changes within any given gait are brought about mainly by means of the half-halt. This puts the horse more onto his haunches, which is the very quintessence of collection. Once you have made the horse relatively more collected, your only other duty is to move in harmony with the modified movement. In general the more collected the gait the easier you will find the motion is to accommodate.

Collection is not primarily about shortening the stride. It is about shifting the weight more onto the haunches, which will incidentally oblige the horse to take shorter, more cadenced steps. When aiding for collection it is important not to take a strong contact on the reins, as this would prevent the horse from taking his weight back. In fact the more collected the gait, the lighter the contact should be.

When schooling the horse to collect himself beyond his normal capacity you will need to use your legs more strongly to increase the engagement of his hindlegs. This leads to the conclusion which would mystify any beginner, that to collect the horse one should use stronger legs and lighter reins! Of course the secret is that you must make sure the horse reacts correctly when you apply your legs. If he tries to go faster, then you should simultaneously tighten your abdomen and thighs as a preventative measure, and maintain a passive resistance with the reins.

Upward transitions

Included in these transitions are changes from one gait to another, and changes within the same gait to a relatively more extended variation. When changing to a different gait it is also possible to ask for more extension at the same time, so one could, for example, change directly from a collected trot to a medium canter.

Halt to walk

The walk is begun by closing your legs against the horse's sides, taking your hips back very slightly so that your lower back flattens and your weight shifts away from the crotch and towards the two seat bones. This should feel more like keeping your hips in place and pushing your seat bones slightly forwards. There should be no obvious pushing or shoving with your seat; the movement need be little more than indicated. Whilst doing this you must keep your shoulders vertically above or slightly behind your hips. You must also yield the reins to allow the horse to move forwards.

If you do not use your seat when applying your legs, then the horse might walk on, but equally he could react just by lowering his head or by collecting himself a little more, or he might even try to step backwards. His reaction will depend on how you are contacting his mouth through the reins.

If you apply your leg and seat aids correctly but resist with the reins, the horse may just collect himself, but the chances are that you will only confuse him and make him tense. Depending on his temperament he might become restive, or he might even rear up.

Walk to trot

To obtain this transition, apply pressure with both legs to the horse's sides and at the same time use your abdominal muscles to stop the motion of your pelvis, which has hitherto been moving to accommodate the gentle motion of the horse's back as he walks along. Allow your weight to act rather more through your seat bones than through your crotch.

The action of the legs should be shorter and slightly more abrupt than when walking on from a standstill, but the pressure applied should not be any stronger. You will not need to do anything with the reins unless something goes wrong. If the horse tries to extend the walk then maintain a passive resistance as you apply the legs and seat, but yield again at the instant the horse moves into a trot.

If you do not inhibit the motion of the walk with your seat, the horse may guess that you want him to remain at the walk and extend the stride. You will then find that to get a trot you need to use your legs more aggressively than is strictly necessary.

Novice riders do not usually know how to use their seat to best advantage during the transition to a trot. This explains why they need to kick their horses with their heels, and why they like to take a firm hold on the reins. The reins prevent the extended walk, and the kicking heels agitate the horse into a trot. It also explains why to them so many horses seem lazy, and why some of them resort to spurs unnecessarily.

Trot to canter

The aids for the canter are issued from a sitting trot. The manner of their application depends on which side you wish the horse to lead. For a right lead canter your left leg must be applied further back than your right leg, in the so-called 'canter position'. If you are turning or circling to the right at the time when you decide to canter, your left leg should already be in the canter position. Do not move it further back, just apply it in that position.

There are disagreements among trainers over which leg the horse should react to. Some say it is the rider's outside leg which causes the strike-off and others say it is the inside one. Nowadays the majority consider the outside leg to be the more important. Certainly when practising flying changes the horse reacts to the new outside leg, but for other canter transitions the truth is that it is possible for the horse to react to either.

On a well schooled horse the canter can be started by applying just the outside leg, whilst holding the inside leg away from his side. Similarly, on the same horse it can also be started by holding the outside leg away from his side and aiding only with the inside leg. Again on the same horse, experiments will show that by holding both legs away from his sides and momentarily increasing the weight through the inside seat bone he will also strike off into canter on the correct lead.

To obtain a smooth transition both legs and the seat will be required. One successful formula is to apply the outside

62

leg first in the canter position to prepare the horse and to signal which lead is required. This is followed immediately by pressure from the inside of the seat, which itself is followed immediately by pressure from the inside leg on the girth.

At the moment of the strike-off into canter it is important that the horse's outside hindleg, which initiates the movement, is not inhibited by the outside rein. For this reason it is the inside rein contact that should dominate when aiding for the canter. Once the canter has been obtained, then provided the horse is sufficiently advanced to be ridden between the inside leg and the outside rein, the contact can be adjusted accordingly.

The aids for the left lead canter are a mirror image of those required for the right lead canter. When asking for a left lead canter it should be very difficult for the horse to strike off onto the right lead, and vice versa. If he does succeed, you should be able to detect the fault before he completes the first stride, and you must immediately bring him back to a trot. Even if the horse is very one-sided and has a preferred leading leg, when you ask for the less favourite lead you should still be able to prevent him from striking off on the wrong lead; he should either lead with the correct leg or not canter at all. Your ability to feel which lead the horse has chosen will depend partly on your experience, and partly on how the horse swings his back. If his back is stiff then it will be much harder to determine what he is doing with his legs.

The trot to canter transition is a difficult one for the novice rider to master. It is not very easy to sit to the trot while applying the canter aids, and the aid required with the seat is itself quite difficult for the beginner to effect. When he fails to obtain the canter he will usually start to use his legs more aggressively, but this will not help the horse to canter. The most likely reaction is that the horse will produce a faster trot. The rider will then pull on the reins, and his riding will disintegrate altogether. Often the problem with this scenario is that the rider is expected to obtain a canter before he has developed an adequate seat. The instructor should be careful to prepare his pupil thoroughly.

Collection to extension

When changing from any gait to a relatively more extended version of the same gait your legs must call for a greater forward thrust from the horse's hind limbs, and the action of your seat must change by moving less vertically and more horizontally, so that it first encourages and then conforms to the new motion of the horse's back. As the cadence decreases the horse's back will swing in a longer form with less amplitude.

At extended walk and trot, provided you have developed a good seat, you will be able to feel quite easily how the two sides of the horse's back move one after the other. As you add energy to the swinging back through your seat you must move each side of your seat alternately in the rhythm of the movement. This of course must be done discretely; there should be no swinging from side to side which could be detected by an observer. At the canter it is the inside of your seat that is responsible for energy input.

The young horse should be allowed to stretch his head and neck forwards and down when lengthening his stride. When teaching the extended trot on a more experienced horse it is a good idea to keep his frame short in the early stages as this will encourage him to stretch out his forelegs to their full extent. Later on, the reins should be yielded slightly to encourage him to lengthen his whole frame.

As the strides are lengthened it is most important that the rhythm remains unchanged. If the rhythm of the footfalls increases it is a sign that the horse is not driving sufficiently from his haunches and that he is not relaxed in his back. He will derive no benefit from the exercise if he is allowed to speed up in this way.

8

STARTING LATERAL WORK

The term 'lateral' is applied to all movements in which the horse moves at an angle to the direction he is facing, rather than straight ahead. Lateral work can be performed either on a straight line or on a circular path. In contrast to single track work the horse's hind feet do not land in the tracks made by his fore feet.

Movements include the *shoulder-in*, the *haunches-in*, the *half-pass*, and the *pirouette*. They are of enormous gymnastic benefit to the horse, being particularly effective in making him strong, supple, and straight, and improving his potential for carrying weight on the haunches.

Most horses are noticeably more pleasant to ride once they have been exercised laterally, so it is important that you incorporate this work into your schooling programme.

Before you can make a start on lateral movements it is essential that your horse moves actively forwards in a relaxed way,

responds correctly to your seat, leg and rein aids, and performs all the simple transitions smoothly. If you start before he can move correctly on a single track then you will only teach him to be evasive, and you may have trouble when you want him to go straight forward. The young horse will not usually be ready to begin lateral work until the end of his first year's training.

When riding lateral movements it is most important that the rhythm and impulsion remain unchanged. The horse must not be allowed to slow down as soon as he starts to move laterally. Young inexperienced horses will be all the more likely to react in this way, and that is another reason why they should not be asked to attempt these exercises too soon.

The shoulder-in is the first lateral exercise to teach the horse, but riders who have not ridden this movement before should start with the turn on the forehand, which is easier to ride.

Turn on the forehand

This exercise can be practised only at the walk, but it can be started either from a walk or from a halt. When turning to the right, the horse must be bent to the right and pivot in a clockwise direction around his right foreleg, which will stay at the centre of the circle. As is usual in a walk the right fore foot must continue to step up and down. It is considered a serious fault if it remains fixed on the ground, because in riding the gaits must always be kept pure. For the turn to the left, the bend would be to the left, and the horse would turn anti-clockwise around his left foreleg.

If the horse has never done any lateral work before, then a good preparation is to teach him to move his quarters over in the stable by pressing a hand against his flank. An extension of the same idea is to work him in hand in the manege. Hold his bridle in one hand, and press the other hand against his side to make him perform a complete turn around the forehand.

The first ridden variation to attempt is the half turn on the forehand starting alongside a wall, turning so that the haunches move inwards away from the wall. Ride on an inner track parallel to the wall so that when negotiating the turn there is plenty of room for the horse's head and shoulders to move out towards the wall.

When riding on the left rein, for example, first change the bend to the right and then halt. Keep your left leg further back than the right, but do not press it against the horse. Look to the right, turn your upper body towards the right, and increase the pressure of your right leg against the girth to encourage the horse to take a step to the left with his right hindleg. If he does not move then try tapping your leg or tapping the whip just behind your leg. If he still will not move then ask someone on the ground to push with his hand.

When helping with his hand the assistant pushes against the ground to make the horse move, but obviously you lose this connection with the ground when you are mounted in the saddle, and the aid loses its element of physical compulsion. Consequently the pressure from your leg is much less effective than that of the assistant's hand, and the exercise is understandably harder to perform.

If the horse tries to evade the exercise by walking directly forwards when you apply your leg then use your seat and reins to prevent him. Do not allow him to walk on and then stop him afterwards, but try to synchronise your aids with the evasion. At the very moment when he tries to walk forwards apply the usual aids for a halt: keeping your back straight close your thighs against the saddle, tighten your abdomen, lean backwards if he is particularly determined to move on, and maintain a passive resistance in the reins.

Under no circumstances must you allow the horse to step backwards. If he tries to do so it is a sure sign that you are holding too much with the reins. Lighten the contact, and use your legs to send him forwards.

When you have mastered the half turn on the forehand to the right, try the half turn to the left, starting with the horse parallel

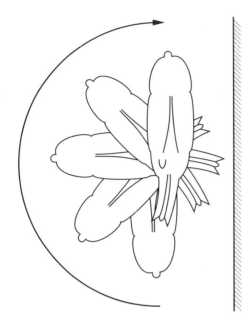

Half turn on the forehand to the right

to the wall. He will probably turn more easily in one direction than the other, and this is just one of the signs of crookedness. Lateral work is particularly effective in alleviating crookedness, so later on when you have mastered the more advanced lateral movements this problem should begin to diminish.

After practising the half turn on the forehand in both directions the next progression is to practise it directly from walk without the preliminary halt. You will need to use a half halt to rebalance the horse and possibly to slow him down if he is rushing, but you should not need to bring him right down to a standstill. This is a typical example of an exercise that is very difficult to perform if the horse is allowed to walk on too briskly. It is very much easier if his speed is kept under control.

The speed during the exercise itself must

be no slower than that of the walk which precedes it. Because the movement demands a different usage of the joints of the hindlegs, most horses that are unfamiliar with the turn on the forehand slow down when they make the turn itself, so they must be encouraged to stay active. You will need to use your inside leg to keep the horse walking in his usual rhythm. Occasionally a horse will rush the turn, and here the outside leg should be used to control the speed, and the exercise must be ridden one step at a time, possibly even halting after each step.

Always perform the exercise without a preparatory halt if you can because then it is easier to maintain the rhythm and to ensure that the horse moves his inside foreleg up and down correctly. After completing the turn maintain the rhythm and allow the horse to walk straight ahead.

The half turn on the forehand need not always be ridden alongside a wall. When working in half the manege, for example, it can be performed when turning across the centre. In this case it is usual to change the bend and turn towards the other half of the school so that the hindquarters remain in your half, and you do not invade another rider's working area.

A complete turn on the forehand is next on the agenda, and this can be performed at any convenient spot in the manege.

Before progressing to the shoulder-in there is one more change which has to be made to the turn on the forehand. Instead of pivoting the horse around the inside foreleg, the forehand must now be allowed to move forwards a little at each step, so

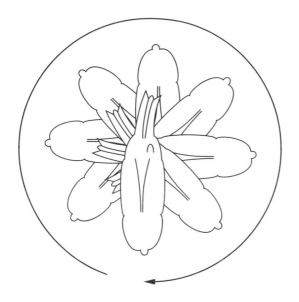

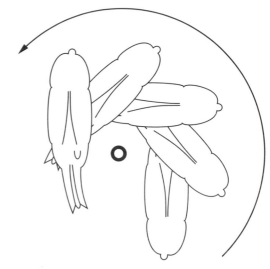

Complete turn on the forehand to the right

Half turn around the forehand to the left

that the inside fore foot describes a small circle on the ground. This is sometimes referred to as a *turn around the forehand*. The easiest way to practise this is to place an object, such as a cone, in the manege at the centre of the circle. For a left turn around the forehand approach the cone with it on your left hand side and commence the turn when the horse's left shoulder is level with the cone. After each step the cone must remain level with his left shoulder.

From now on this is the manner in which the exercise should be ridden. Because of the forward movement this variation is superior to the pivot on the spot. It reduces the risk of the horse evading by stepping backwards, and it enables the inside hindleg to engage forwards under the weight a little more. You should also find it easier to maintain the rhythm and the bend to the inside, and you should be able

to lighten the contact on the inside rein without losing the bend. Yielding the inside rein and keeping a contact on the outside rein will free the horse's inside shoulder and also allow his inside hindleg to engage more easily. Naturally, if you lose the bend you will need to take up the contact on the inside rein again in order to recover it.

The turn on the forehand is not in itself a particularly valuable exercise. It is really the novice rider's stepping stone to the shoulder-in, which is far more beneficial to the horse, but which is not quite so easy to ride. The main disadvantage of the turn on the forehand is that the inside hindleg is obliged to move too much sideways and not enough forwards, so it does not participate sufficiently in weight support. In fact it encourages the weight to be transferred towards the shoulders rather than the hindquarters. Another disadvantage is that it can only be practised at the walk, which does not exercise the horse sufficiently. For these reasons it cannot be considered to be a classical movement.

Another exercise which cannot be counted as classical is the *leg-yield*. Although this is currently rather fashionable, it is actually a disengaging exercise which cannot contribute constructively to the long term physical development of the horse. Considering that the shoulder-in is available and is far superior in its influence on the horse, the leg-yield is a rather pointless exercise. Any newcomer to lateral work will find it quite easy to learn the shoulder-in after practising the progression of exercises described above, and any experienced rider will be able to start directly with the shoulder-in. It is not necessary to learn the academically unsound leg-yield, and consequently instruction in this dubious exercise is not included here.

Shoulder-in

Having mastered some lateral control of the haunches by using the turn on the forehand, you will be ready to learn the shoulder-in and the shoulder-out.

These two exercises are functionally equivalent. In the shoulder-in to the right, for example, the horse works alongside a wall on his left side, keeping his haunches on the track, and the rider brings his forehand in away from the wall. In the shoulder-out to the right the horse works with his haunches on an inner track alongside a wall on his right, and the rider takes his shoulders out towards the wall.

As the drawings below show, there are different degrees of shoulder-in. In the shoulder-fore, the forehand is brought in slightly so that the horse's withers are positioned directly in front of his inside hindleg. In the three-track shoulder-in, the withers are taken in further until the

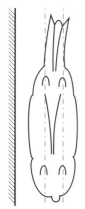

Horse positioned right moving straight ahead

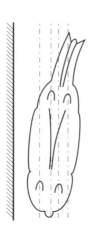

Shoulder-fore

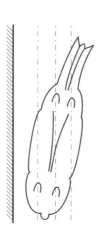

Three track shoulder-in

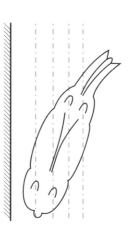

Four track shoulder-in

outside foreleg is directly in front of the inside hindleg. In the four-track version, the shoulders are taken in further still so that the outside fore foot makes a new track beyond that made by the inside hind foot.

The shoulder-in is valuable for two reasons. Firstly the motion of the forelimbs and shoulders has the effect of making the horse more pliant. A supple horse is a safe horse, so suppleness is considered to be a major requirement in a good riding horse. Secondly, because of the lateral bend and the direction of movement, the horse engages his inside hindleg well under his body, and it carries and propels a greater proportion of weight than normal. This strengthens the hock and contributes to the overall aims of schooling by putting the horse more on his haunches.

Although it is more usual to practise shoulder-in and shoulder-out alongside a wall, they can also be ridden on any straight line away from a wall, or on a circle. When learning to write one uses lined paper to help keep the script straight and tidy. The wall has a similar function in riding: it assists one to keep the horse on the proper track when attempting an unfamiliar exercise, so the exercises should be mastered alongside a wall before the other variations are attempted.

One advantage of working on a circle is that the flow of the exercise is never interrupted by meeting corners. The circle is usually more convenient if you are working in a small manege where all the sides are short, or if you have only half the school available. Shoulder-in should not be practised through tight turns or on small circles because it puts too much weight on the forehand and restricts the horse's movement, making it very difficult for him to turn.

Practice at the turn on the forehand is a good preparation for learning to ride the shoulder-in despite the fact that the horse moves somewhat differently in the two patterns. When riding the turn around the forehand on a small circle the horse's forelegs move directly forwards at each step and his haunches move laterally, the inside hindleg stepping across in front of the outside hindleg. At shoulder-in, however, the haunches do not move so much sideways. The inside hindleg steps further under the body than usual, but it does not appear to cross over the outside hindleg. The shoulders progress laterally, the inside foreleg stepping across in front of the outside one.

The four-track shoulder-in is the best one to aim for when you are learning to ride the movement. If you try for one of the lesser angled varieties you are likely to succeed only in bringing the head and neck in, and the horse will continue to progress straight ahead along the track. The walk is the gait to use for teaching the horse how to move at shoulder-in. Later on you can practise at the trot, and this will have a very beneficial effect on the horse's development.

The shoulder-out is often easier to ride than the shoulder-in, because the wall prevents the horse from stepping directly forwards. When attempting the exercise for the first time one of the easiest approaches is to develop it from the turn on the forehand. For the shoulder-out to the right, walk along an inner track on the right rein, parallel to the long side of the manege, which should be on your left. On approaching the corner ride a half turn around the forehand to the right, so that you are facing the opposite direction. Ride one extra step so that the horse is at an angle to the wall. Hold the left rein to prevent the horse walking directly forwards towards the wall, and increase the pressure from your right leg on the girth. Keep your left leg behind the girth, and this will help to distribute your weight more over towards the right side of your seat. Yield the right rein to allow the horse to move his right shoulder and cross his right foreleg over sideways towards the left.

If the horse does walk forwards to the wall and starts to straighten up, then correct his position by riding one or two steps of a turn on the forehand to the right. You cannot afford to be a passenger; you will have to be in control of every step and make appropriate adjustments, because the horse is certain to find the movement difficult at first, and he will try to evade your instructions if he can. After a few successful steps, straighten up and allow the horse to relax on a long rein as a reward before making an attempt on the other rein.

The shoulder-in can also be generated from a half turn on the forehand. For a shoulder-in to the right, ride on an inner track on the left rein, parallel to the long side of the manege. On approaching the corner, bend

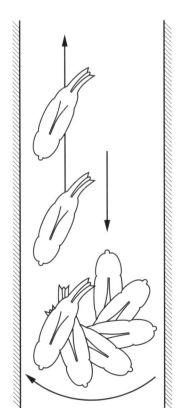

Left: The shoulder-in and shoulder-out can both be generated from the turn around the forehand.

The drawing shows two walls, to indicate that the exercise can be positioned by either one or the other.

When positioned by the wall on the left, the shoulder-in is produced, but when placed near the wall on the right the exercise becomes a shoulder-out.

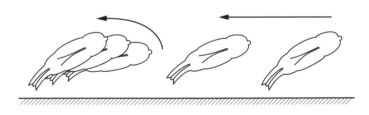

Above: If the horse straightens up to evade the shoulder-out to the left, then correct his position by riding a step or two of a turn on the forehand to the left.

the horse to the right and ride a half turn around the forehand to the right, moving the haunches away from your right leg. Ride one extra step to set the horse at an angle to the wall then use your right leg to send him sideways along the wall. Yield the right rein to give freedom to his right shoulder and foreleg. Keep a contact on the left rein to discourage him from walking in away from the wall. He may drift in away from the wall at first until his right hindleg gets stronger. Do not pull on the reins to prevent this drift, but ride a

circle and start another shoulder-in. If the inward drift proves difficult to control then practise shoulder-out instead of shoulder-in.

When you have succeeded in starting shoulder-in and shoulder-out from a turn on the forehand, try starting a shoulder-in after turning through a corner and riding a volte (a small circle). In this case you would ride along the next wall in shoulder-in. Try starting a shoulder-out after turning through a corner and riding a half volte. In

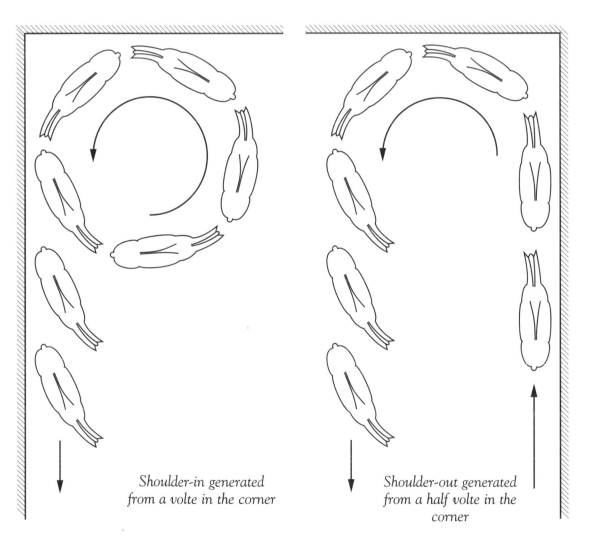

Shoulder-in generated
from a volte in the corner

Shoulder-out generated
from a half volte in the
corner

this case you would return in shoulder-out along the wall which led to the corner. Once you can successfully start the exercises in this fashion you will rarely need to use the turn on the forehand again.

Now is the time to practise shoulder-in and shoulder-out at a collected trot. After trying the movements alongside the wall, try them on straight lines away from the wall, and on a large circle. The disadvantage of using the wall is that the horse does not react solely to your aids, but also gains support from the wall.

A volte inside a large circle would be a good preparation for the shoulder-in on a large circle, whilst a volte ridden outside a circle would enable you to change the bend and prepare for the shoulder-out. If you are feeling adventurous you can try riding more sophisticated patterns at the shoulder-in. A serpentine, for example, would give you the opportunity to try both the shoulder-in and the shoulder-out.

At trot it is very difficult to make adjustments if you lose the horse's position. It is invariably necessary to start a new shoulder-in when this happens, after first establishing a bend in the required direction by riding a volte.

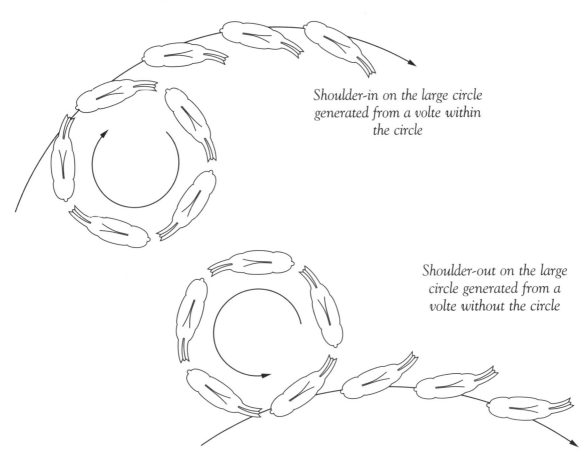

Shoulder-in on the large circle generated from a volte within the circle

Shoulder-out on the large circle generated from a volte without the circle

At canter the horse is capable of maintaining only a slight shoulder-in, or 'shoulder-fore' position. This is known as the *plié* canter. When ridden alongside a wall the plié is a useful correction for the horse who allows his haunches to drift in at canter. It can also be used by advanced riders as a preparation for the canter pirouette.

One of the most useful forms of the plié is to turn down the centre line and to ride the plié on a diagonal line out towards the wall on the side opposite to the leading

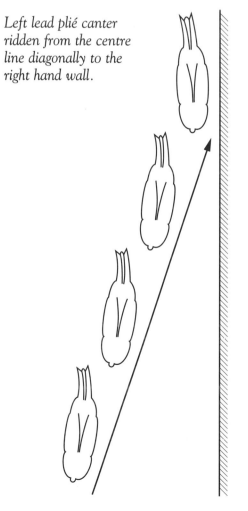

Left lead plié canter ridden from the centre line diagonally to the right hand wall.

leg. Another beneficial exercise is to spiral inwards at canter from a large circle down to a small circle and to use the plié to move the horse laterally out onto the large circle again.

Haunches-in

Once you and your horse can manage the shoulder-in without any difficulty, the time has arrived to attempt the haunches-in. This is also known as *quarters-in*, or *travers*. It is usually, but not necessarily, ridden on the track alongside a wall. The forehand remains on the track and, as the name suggests, the haunches are kept on an inner track by means of the rider's outside leg applied behind the girth.

When the haunches-in is ridden on a straight line the horse must look straight ahead along the track. His forelegs will not cross, but at walk and trot his outside hind foot will move over to a position below the inner half of his body so that when viewed from behind his tail the hindlegs will appear to cross. At canter the horse bounds sideways without crossing his legs.

Haunches-in alongside a wall

At haunches-in the outside hindleg has a greater share in responsibility for propelling the horse along, whilst the inside hindleg, which must stay well engaged and not step in to the side, has an important function in weight support.

As is usual with any new movement it is best at first to practise haunches-in at the walk, although it is more effective in its influence on the horse when ridden at the trot. For haunches-in to the right, as you enter a corner on the right rein, ride a volte, keeping the walk slow and controlled, and making sure the horse is properly bent to the right. As you emerge from the corner after completing the volte, use your left leg behind the girth to encourage the horse to step sideways with his hindquarters. Keep the contact on the right rein otherwise the horse will lose his bend to the right. Do not lean over to the left, but keep your body upright with slightly more weight on the right side of your seat. Yield the left rein in time with the movement to allow the horse to move his outside shoulder and foreleg. For the first few attempts do nothing with your right leg or you will only confuse the horse.

At first you should be content if you can ride just three or four steps moving diagonally forwards and sideways. At this stage it does not matter very much if the movement does not resemble a perfect haunches-in. The first task is to learn how to control the haunches. You can tidy it up into a classic haunches-in when lateral control of the haunches becomes easier.

When you can ride the exercise equally well on both reins at the walk, and it is beginning to take shape reasonably well, then try the movement at a trot. Ride a volte in collected trot in a corner of the manege, and start the haunches-in as you emerge from the corner. If you lose the movement then circle again and make another attempt, reapplying the aids just before you return to the wall.

You might now discover that you need to apply some pressure with your inside leg on the girth to keep the horse properly bent to the inside, and to prevent his inside hindleg from stepping sideways too far. Later on when your horse has thoroughly mastered the exercise and your inside leg is effective in keeping his inside hindleg well

Haunches-in generated from a volte

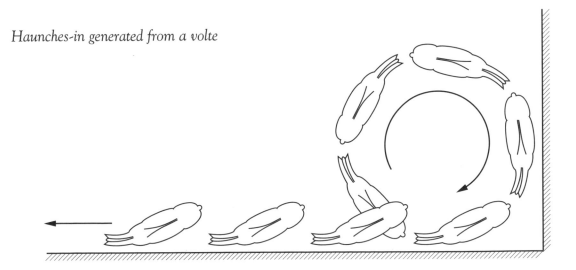

engaged you can yield the inside rein. With an advanced horse this should not result in losing the bend, and you can allow him to take a contact on the outside rein instead. The lighter contact on the inside rein will itself assist the engagement of the inside hindleg. If you find that you do lose the bend then you will have no option but to revert to using the inside rein contact again.

When you have finished riding haunches-in along the wall do not not push the hindquarters sideways out onto the track to terminate the exercise, as that would have a disengaging effect. Since the horse is already bent on the arc of a circle, all you need to do is to ride as though you were completing the circle, and straighten up to ride along the track.

Another way to terminate the haunches-in is to bring the horse's shoulders in and place them directly in front of his haunches. In this case the horse will finish a short distance in from the track.

When you are confident that you can ride haunches-in along the wall there are a number of other variations that you can attempt. The first is to practise the exercise a little further from the wall so that the forehand travels on an inner track. Make sure you keep the horse parallel to the wall all the way along.

The next variation is haunches-in down the centre line. You can use the turn to prepare yourself and your horse, or you can ride a volte first if you need a little longer to establish the bending. After that you should have no difficulty in riding the exercise along any straight line you wish, and you will be ready to attempt it on the large circle. This can be prepared by riding a volte within the circle.

The haunches-in can be ridden at the

Terminating the haunches-in by riding an arc of a circle

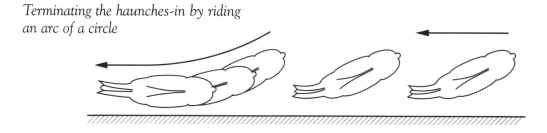

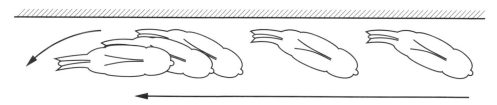

Terminating the haunches-in by placing the shoulders in front of the haunches

canter, but it is not advisable to ride it along the wall. At canter all horses are inclined to swing their hindquarters inwards, though sadly not in a correct haunches-in; they step in sideways with the inside hindleg so that it cannot carry the weight properly. Because it is easier for the rider to control the engagement of the inside hindleg at the half-pass than it is at the haunches-in, it a good idea to shelve the haunches-in at canter until you have mastered the half-pass.

Half-pass

The half-pass is a similar movement to the haunches-in, but the horse is ridden at a steeper angle so that at walk and trot his outside foreleg is obliged to cross over in front of his inside foreleg. As with the haunches-in the legs do not cross at canter. The horse must remain slightly bent

towards the direction of travel, but he no longer moves in the direction in which his nose is pointing. Usually the half-pass is ridden on a diagonal line across the arena, but this is by no means essential. You can ride it on any straight line, and on a large circle too, with either the tail or the head towards the centre.

As with the haunches-in, unless you have an advanced horse you will need to use your outside leg to move the horse sideways, and you will need the contact on the inside rein to keep him bent in the proper direction.

For your first attempt at the half-pass it is a good idea to ride it alongside a wall in much the same way as you rode the haunches-in. Ride a circle or a corner to establish the proper bend before you start. Try it at first at a walk and then at a trot. You will need to keep slightly farther away

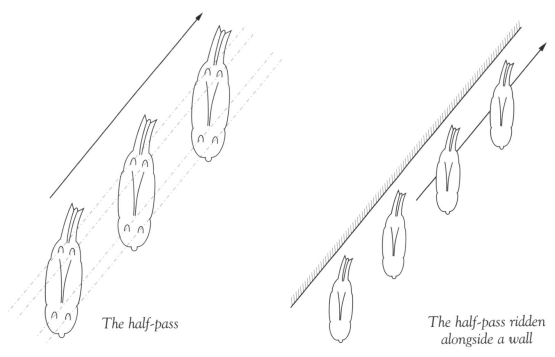

The half-pass

The half-pass ridden alongside a wall

from the wall than when riding haunches-in, so as to avoid scraping the horse's nose or knees.

Having practised the exercise along the wall, try riding a half volte out of a corner and returning to the track in half-pass. This time the horse will be reacting only to your aids, as he will no longer have the assistance of the wall. This is a better test of your lateral control of the horse. Try the half volte and half-pass at canter too. As you become more proficient you can enlarge the half volte so that you increase the distance to be covered in half-pass. Ultimately you will be able to ride through

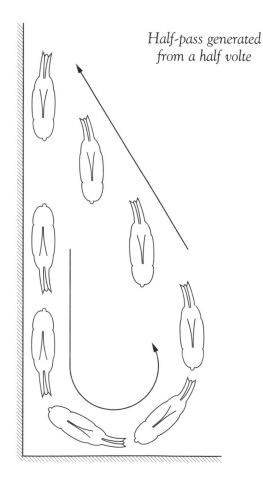

*Half-pass generated
from a half volte*

a corner and ride a half-pass along the whole length of the diagonal.

As with the haunches-in, the horse's inside hindleg must remain well engaged and not step in sideways. This fault is more noticeable at the half-pass because it causes the horse to lead with his haunches instead of his shoulders. Leading with the haunches is not a totally reliable indicator of a faulty half-pass. Related to the half-pass is a movement known as the *full pass* in which the horse moves directly sideways. This is usually ridden sideways across the arena, but should it be ridden along the diagonal it would appear to an observer as a half-pass with the haunches leading, yet it would not be a faulty movement.

The shoulder-in is a particularly good preparation for the half-pass because it ensures the proper engagement of the inside hindleg. If you feel you are losing the engagement a good correction is to ride a few steps of shoulder-in before restarting the half-pass.

When you have mastered the half-pass at canter you should be sufficiently in control of the haunches to make a good attempt at the haunches-in at canter. Practise this on the centre line, along the diagonal, and on the large circle. Make sure you keep the inside hindleg well engaged.

Full pass

This exercise is effectively a half-pass in which the forward progression is reduced to a minimum so that the horse moves directly sideways. It is a difficult movement to ride at trot or canter, and it requires a very well trained horse. At the walk, however, it is surprisingly easy to ride, and although it does not have any great gymnastic merit, it is a useful test of your ability to manœuvre the horse.

The aids are the same as those used for the half-pass, except that a passive resistance in the reins prevents the horse from gaining ground to the front should he try to do so.

Full pass to the left

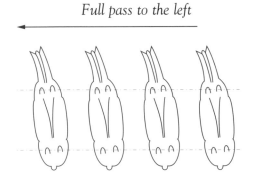

Haunches-out

Haunches-out is also known as *quarters-out*, *renvers*, or *tail to the wall*. It is functionally equivalent to haunches-in,

but here the forehand moves straight ahead along an inner track, whilst the haunches are kept out on the track by the rider's outside leg, which in this case is the leg nearer to the centre of the school. Haunches-out is arguably a more useful exercise than haunches-in, because the horse is influenced less by the wall, and reacts more to the rider's aids.

One way to prepare the haunches-out would be to ride down the long side of the manege, ride a half volte in the corner and then return almost to the track in half-pass. On approaching the track push the haunches out to the track with your outside leg, and ride back along the long side of the arena in haunches-out. Before reaching the corner, straighten up your horse by taking his shoulders out to the track. If you are riding at canter you could continue after the exercise in counter-canter, or you could change to another gait.

Haunches-out on the circle is one of the most difficult lateral exercises to ride. It can be prepared by riding a volte outside a large circle and then continuing around the circle in the haunches-out position.

Haunches-out generated from a half-pass

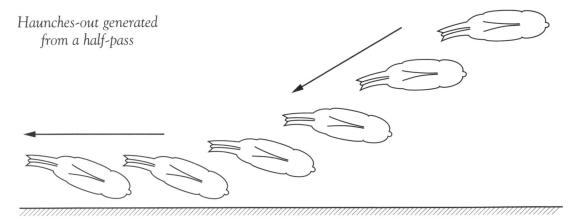

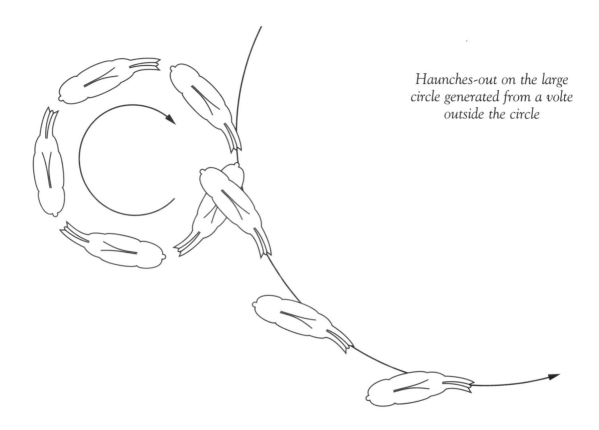

Haunches-out on the large circle generated from a volte outside the circle

Walk pirouette

In the walk pirouette the horse makes a 360° turn around his inside hind foot, which steps up and down on the spot. It is an extremely difficult movement to ride well, and strictly speaking is an exercise for the advanced horse and the advanced rider.

It is very important that the horse retains the purity of the walk and the rhythm. It is all too easy to allow him to cease stepping with his inside hindleg, to step backwards, or to slow down during the turn.

Before attempting the pirouette itself, a good exercise to practise is a volte with the

croup to the centre. This is ridden as a half-pass around a very small circle, and differs from the normal half-pass only in that in order to navigate the turn the forelegs cross much more than usual and the hindlegs cross much less than usual. For this exercise you may find it helps if you set up a cone or some other convenient object at the centre of the circle. You can keep your eye on this and use it as a reference point.

For a turn around the haunches to the left, approach the cone with it on your left hand side and start the turn when the horse's hindquarters are level with it. Relative to you the cone should appear in exactly the same position as you ride all

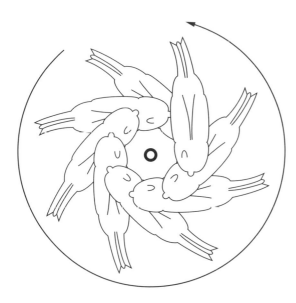

Turn around the haunches to the left, the centre of the circle marked by a cone

position. Ride shoulder-out to the left on an inner track parallel to the long side of the manege with the wall on your left. On reaching the corner attempt a half turn to the left and return along the same long side in shoulder-in. Be sure, during the turn, to use your inside leg in the rhythm of the movement to keep the horse stepping with his inside hindleg.

When you are successful with the half walk pirouette in the corner of the school you can attempt a three-quarter pirouette and continue along the short side of the

the way round. Keep the horse moving smartly forwards and sideways at each step.

When you can ride the turn around the haunches in both directions you will be ready to attempt the half pirouette. This is ridden in the same way as the turn around the haunches except that the circle around which you turn is reduced to a tiny circle a few inches in diameter, so there will be no room for the cone.

At first you will need the help of the walls of the school; you will have little hope of success if you make your first attempt in the middle of nowhere. Since the horse needs to keep his inside hindleg well engaged during the turn it is a good plan to use the shoulder-in or the shoulder-out as a preparation.

One good approach would be to aim for a half pirouette starting from a shoulder-out

Half walk pirouette to the left generated from a shoulder-out

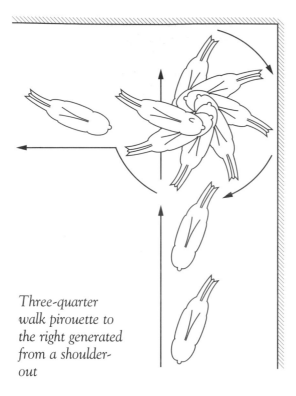

Three-quarter walk pirouette to the right generated from a shoulder-out

Suggested progression of exercises to practise

In-hand work

1. Move the quarters over in the stable by pressing a hand against the flank

2. Work in hand in the manege, holding the bridle in one hand and making the horse do a complete turn on the forehand by pressing the other hand against his flank

Ridden work

3. Half turn on the forehand against a wall, starting from a halt, with an assistant to help by pressing a hand against the flank if necessary

4. Half turn on the forehand against a wall, staying in walk, without halting

5. Half turn on the forehand away from the wall

6. Complete turn on the forehand

7. Turn around the forehand, working round a central cone

8. Shoulder-out at walk, developed from a half turn around the forehand

9. Shoulder-in at walk, developed from a half turn around the forehand

10. Shoulder-in at walk, developed from a volte

11. Shoulder-out at walk, developed from a half volte

manege in shoulder-out. You could make another attempt in the next corner.

Now you will be ready to try the half pirouette alongside a wall. To make the turn easier, ride one or two steps of shoulder-in as a preparation, then turn the horse inwards away from the wall. When you have mastered this try a half turn or a full turn starting on a straight line away from the wall.

Sometimes it is easier for the rider to make the horse turn when riding a turn on the haunches, which differs from the pirouette only in that it is started from a halt. It is, however, usually harder to achieve a good quality movement because the flow and the rhythm of the walk are interrupted.

12. Shoulder-in and shoulder-out at trot

13. Shoulder-in at trot on a straight line away from the wall

14. Shoulder-out and shoulder-in on the large circle at trot

15. Plié canter

16. Haunches-in at walk, developed from a volte

17. Haunches-in at trot, developed from a volte

18. Haunches-in at walk and trot, at a distance from, but parallel to the wall

19. Haunches-in at trot on the centre line

20. Haunches-in at trot on the large circle

21. Half-pass alongside a wall at walk

22. Half-pass alongside a wall at trot

23. Half-pass at trot on a short diagonal, and on the main diagonal

24. Half-pass at canter on a short diagonal, and on the main diagonal

25. Haunches-in at canter on the centre line, the main diagonal, and the large circle

26. Full pass at walk

27. Haunches-out at walk, trot, and canter, developed from a half-pass

28. Haunches-out on the large circle at walk, trot and canter

29. Turn around the haunches at walk, working round a central cone

30. Half walk pirouette in a corner, starting from shoulder-out

31. Three-quarter walk pirouette in a corner, starting from shoulder-out

32. Half walk pirouette alongside the wall, starting from shoulder-in

33. Half walk pirouette away from the wall

34. Full walk pirouette

9

DIRECT TRANSITIONS

Learning to ride direct transitions will be a major breakthrough in perfecting your skill in the saddle, and will add enormously to the effectiveness of your aids.

The aids required are much the same as those used for the simple transitions. The main difference is that more effort must be put into preparing the horse by adjusting his deportment, balance, and impulsion, until he is moving in such a way that he can perform the required transition easily. Some exposure to lateral work will usually give him sufficient suppleness, strength, and balance to be able to cope without too much trouble.

Direct upward transitions are very effective in strengthening the hindquarters, and even novice horses will find them immensely beneficial gymnastic exercises.

Direct downward transitions are effective in shifting the horse's weight back, which helps to make him more collected and better balanced.

If you are not experienced at riding direct transitions then you should leave them until you and your horse have mastered the lateral exercises, when you will both find they are much easier. If you are already adept at riding direct transitions you will probably be able to introduce them to the horse you are currently schooling somewhat earlier. If you are inexperienced, you will also find that the upward transitions are easier to produce than the downward ones, so you should try the upward ones first. In dressage competitions the direct upward transitions are required at a lower level than the downward ones.

Once you have mastered the direct downward transitions you will find that most horses have no difficulty with them, and it is quite in order to teach these before the upward transitions. In fact this strategy will improve the horse's balance so that the upward transitions become more readily available.

At first you should keep your horse in

collection, but as you become more proficient you will be able to attempt changes to and from the medium and extended paces too. Eventually you should even be able to manage changes such as extended trot to collected walk, or halt to medium canter, fairly easily.

Be particularly attentive to the quality of the transitions. Adjust your seat, leg and rein aids as necessary to make them as smooth as possible. It is important to continue to practise the simple transitions too, otherwise the horse is liable to anticipate the direct transitions and produce them regardless of your aids.

Upward transitions

Halt to trot

This is the first direct upward transition for the horse to learn. You should not need to use your legs any more strongly than when trotting from a walk, but the leg action should be more abrupt than when moving off from a halt into a walk. You will need to hold your abdominal muscles firm as you aid with the legs, otherwise the horse may move off at a walk. A tap with the schooling whip may be helpful on the first few occasions.

The horse will find it very difficult to trot on unless the halt is well balanced and square. Frequent transitions between walk and trot, and trot and canter, will help keep the horse attentive to the aids, and will prepare him well for the halt to trot transition. Do not remain long at the halt or the horse will lose his collection and will find it harder to spring forwards.

Walk to canter

The walk to canter transition is easier to ride than the trot to canter transition, because the walk is easier to sit to than the trot, and it is consequently easier to control the application of the aids. The direct transition is a little harder for the horse, because it demands that he is better balanced with more weight on his haunches. There is a knack in preparing the horse so that he is ready to move into canter the moment you apply the aids. With the benefit of a good preparation most horses can perform the transition very easily. Mastery of walk to canter transitions indicates that you have good control of the placement of the horse's hind feet on the ground.

The horse strikes off into canter when his outside fore foot is on the ground, so this is the ideal time to apply the aids. If you have trouble synchronising the aids with the horse's movement you should still be successful, but you must expect a delayed response.

When teaching this transition you can make it easier for the horse by first collecting his walk. If he can already change down directly to walk from canter then you could ride one of these transitions and strike off into canter again shortly after arriving at the walk. If you decide to strike off on the opposite lead, you will be riding a 'simple change of lead'.

Another good preparation is to give the horse a shoulder-fore position at the walk before asking for the canter, to improve the engagement of his inside hindleg. Riding a small circle in collected trot, halting, walking on for two or three steps and then going immediately into canter is another way to improve the collection. There are endless possibilities.

For the transition to be considered successful the horse must move directly into canter without so much as a single intermediate step of trot.

Halt to canter

The aids for this transition are applied in the same manner, and with no greater intensity than for any other canter strike-off. The transition is very easy to ride provided the horse is properly prepared. Naturally he must be well trained, or he will not be able to do it. He must be able to collect himself well so that he is ready to spring forwards from engaged hindlegs.

The horse will not manage the transition unless is already adept at cantering directly from a walk. He will find it much easier if you practise some collecting exercises first. For horses that can already execute direct downward transitions, either canter to halt or trot to halt would be a very good preparation. The quality of the halt is critical: the horse must be collected and square. Regardless of how you arrive at the halt, attempt to move off at canter almost immediately while the horse still carries enough weight on his haunches.

You must ensure that the horse moves directly into canter on the required lead. If you allow even one step of walk or trot then you will have failed.

Downward transitions

Trot to halt

For your first attempt at trot to halt, ride a small circle close to a wall at a collected trot. If you apply the aids for the halt as you approach the wall you will be more likely to succeed. Use the same aids for halting as you would when stopping from a walk, but use your legs to keep the horse well collected. Hold your pelvis still by keeping your abdominal muscles firm, and be prepared to lean backwards on the first few occasions until you are successful.

Soon you will be able to sit upright in the correct position and stop the horse directly, but in the early stages you will find that leaning back as you ask for the halt greatly increases the effectiveness of your aids. It is the best way to discover the stopping power of your seat. Many riders never develop the use of their seat as an aid because they are too concerned about maintaining the ideal upright posture. If you try to remain upright and the transition proves difficult you will be tempted to tighten the reins, which will bring about an abrupt jolting halt with the horse on the forehand.

If the horse puts in some steps of walk before he stops then try riding a smaller circle, and try using your legs a little more to engage his hindlegs further under his body. If you still find the transition elusive then try halting from a shoulder-in or from a half pass. Both of these exercises help to engage the hindlegs, and consequently the horse will be well prepared for stopping.

Although a well planned preparation will

make the transition much easier for the horse, it cannot entirely substitute for lack of skill on the part of the rider. If the horse manages to walk before stopping the fault undoubtedly lies in your seat, which is ineffective in its ability to prevent motion in the horse. Do not imagine that you have mastered the transition until you can pass directly from a trot to a halt without a single intermediate step of walk. The horse must also come to rest at a square halt.

Halting from the medium or extended trot can look quite spectacular. In fact these halts are surprisingly easy to ride. It is stopping from a fast unbalanced trot that is difficult. The transition involves using the half halt to change to a collected pace immediately before halting. With practice the horse will collect himself very quickly, and it should not take longer than three strides to bring him smoothly to a standstill from the moment you decide to stop.

Canter to walk

When riding this transition for the first time, prepare for it in the same way that you did when riding trot to halt: work in a collected canter on a small circle positioned close to a wall, and apply the aids as you approach the wall. Again, you will find that leaning back as you ask for the walk will make the exercise noticeably easier at first. Later on, as your seat becomes more effective you will be able to bring about the transition while sitting

upright in the proper position.

The aids for the transition are similar to those used for changing down to a trot, except that you must hold your pelvis still so that the horse cannot proceed in trot.

Once you have mastered this exercise you will be surprised how easy it is. You will find that horses you had previously thought would never be able to walk directly from a canter can manage it quite easily, and you will scarcely know what it is that you are doing to bring about the transition. Of course this has nothing to do with the training of the horses, it is merely that you are learning to be more effective in applying your aids.

Canter to halt

Surprisingly, halting from a canter is often easier to ride than halting from a trot, probably because the horse naturally engages his hindlegs more at the canter. The aids are much the same as those used to bring the horse down to a walk, but they must persist long enough to prevent the horse from walking on. Again you will find that leaning back and working on a small circle beside a wall will help in the early stages.

At first it will be sufficient if the horse stops directly without taking any walk steps, but later the quality of the halt will also be important, and he will have to come to rest at a square halt.

10

COUNTER-CANTER AND REIN-BACK

These two exercises are grouped together here for two reasons: firstly they both help to strengthen the horse's lower back, and secondly it is appropriate to start riding both of them at around the same stage in the horse's training, as soon as he has learned the lateral movements and the direct transitions.

Although the exercises are valuable gymnastically, neither of them is particularly pleasing to the eye. The counter-canter is inclined to look awkward, rather as if the horse is cantering on the wrong lead by mistake, and because he is rarely seen moving backwards, the rein-back can make him seem restive even though he is stepping back willingly at the command of his rider.

The counter-canter

The counter-canter is either a left lead canter in which the horse turns to the right, or a right lead canter in which he turns to the left. Strictly speaking there is no such thing as a counter-canter on a straight line, but sometimes a canter leading with the leg on the same side as the wall is also referred to as a counter-canter.

When learning to ride the counter-canter it is best to start at the true canter and then turn onto a large arc in the other direction. The easiest pattern to ride is a shallow loop along the long side of the manege. The beginning and end of the loop will be ridden at the true canter, but the horse will be in counter-canter throughout the central portion.

Ride at working canter or collected canter and keep the horse bent in the direction of his leading leg. Keep the leg on the outside of the bend well behind the girth, and keep the inside of your seat pressed well down into the saddle. Do not allow the horse to speed up and enlarge the pattern, or the gymnastic benefit of the exercise will be lost.

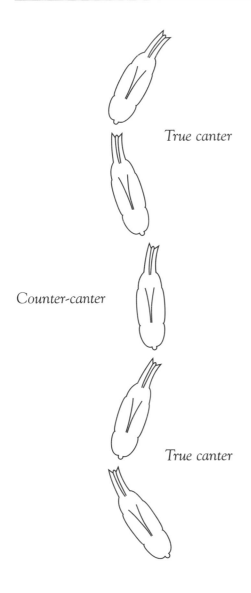

True canter

Counter-canter

True canter

Counter-canter is a tiring exercise for the horse, and so the demands must be increased gradually. As you and your horse become more proficient you will be able to negotiate deeper loops and tighter turns with greater ease, and the patterns will help to increase the horse's capacity for collection. Eventually you should be able to ask for a strike off directly into counter-canter without having to start at the true canter. Bend the horse in the direction of the required leading leg before you ask for the transition. Remember you can initiate a canter from a halt, a walk, or a trot.

The rein-back

To help the horse to step backwards, adjust your seat by tilting your pelvis slightly forwards so that your weight shifts away from the seat bones and towards the crotch. Apply a constant pressure with both legs after sliding them a few inches farther back than usual, and at the same time offer a passive resistance through the reins to prevent the horse from walking forwards. As he steps back relax the rein contact.

For the first few attempts you may find it helps if you exaggerate the influence of your seat by leaning the upper body forward slightly. If the horse is still reluctant to move then ask an assistant to help by pressing a hand against the horse's breast, or by tapping him lightly on this spot with a stick.

Do not pull on the reins. This cannot help the horse to move in any direction because moving will not enable him to relieve the pressure on his mouth.

If you have a large field available for schooling then the exercise will be even easier. Ride a circle in true canter, and when you are ready to attempt the counter-canter, change onto a very large circle in the other direction. You can change back to the original direction at any time and ride another circle in true canter. Always revert to the true canter before the counter-canter disintegrates.

The horse must not creep back dragging his feet, which he might do if you pull on the reins, and neither must he rush back out of control. Never allow him to realise that he can evade your forward driving aids by running backwards. If he moves too quickly you can retard his progress by tilting your pelvis back to its normal position, and by leaning back until your shoulders are behind the line of your hips.

The horse must step smartly backwards in a straight line, moving one diagonal pair of legs after the other, and he should be ready to move forwards again without any delay. Four to six steps of rein-back will be quite sufficient, after which you should move off straight away at a walk, a trot, or a canter.

Rein-back to walk

To arrest the backward motion, close your thighs against the saddle, release the pressure of your legs against the horse's sides and slide them forwards a few inches to their normal position. At the same time tilt your pelvis back to its normal position, flattening your back a little so that your weight shifts away from the crotch and towards the seat bones.

To walk forwards, yield the reins, relax the thighs, and reapply the pressure with your legs.

Rein-back to trot

In reality this is a rein-back to halt followed immediately by a halt to trot transition. First arrest the backward motion in exactly the same way as when riding a rein-back to walk transition, and then promptly apply the aids for a halt to trot. When properly ridden the rein-back sets the horse on his haunches and helps him to spring forwards into the trot, so it should be an easier transition to ride than the halt to trot.

Rein-back to canter

One would perhaps expect this to be the most difficult of all the transitions, but as with the rein-back to trot transition, the backward motion helps to prepare the horse for the canter by setting him more on his haunches, so he is ready to spring forwards whenever you ask him to. The normal canter aids are used, after the backward movement has been arrested.

Ride the transition as a rein-back to halt, followed immediately by a halt to canter. You can prepare for the impending canter while you are arresting the backward movement, by keeping your outside leg back in the 'canter position' so you are ready to apply the canter aids with the minimum delay.

11

SCHOOL PATTERNS

Going large around the arena is the most basic pattern of all. The wall is particularly useful when schooling young horses because it helps to keep them moving on a straight line.

All the corners must be ridden as quarter circles. Novice horses will only manage large sweeping arcs through the corners, as they will be unable to bend sufficiently to negotiate tight turns.

Halving the school provides an opportunity for keeping on a straight line away from the wall. It is important that the horse can move straight when directed only by the aids, without the assistance of the wall.

The *large circle* is the easiest of many exercises which promote lateral bending. Negotiating a true circle, whilst being very important, will usually be the least of your problems. Keeping the horse correctly bent and carrying himself properly will be much harder to achieve. Experienced riding masters make great use of the circle as they

find the pattern is sufficient to yield to them all the horse's imperfections, which they can then correct. Novice riders usually have to attempt more complex

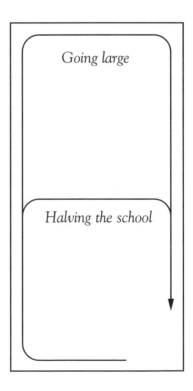

Going large

Halving the school

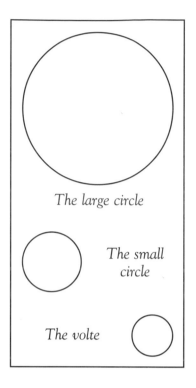

The large circle

The small circle

The volte

and a smaller circle at trot than he can at canter. Since one side is usually more stiff than the other you may also notice that he can manage smaller circles on one rein than he can on the other.

The **volte** is the smallest circle that the horse will ever be able to describe. Its radius is defined as the length of the horse. In the past this rather vague quantity was estimated at 8 feet. Nowadays somewhat larger horses are fashionable and our voltes are generally larger, although obviously a volte for a pony would be considerably smaller than that for a large horse. Only a very well schooled supple horse will be able to turn easily around a volte.

The definition of the volte has been subject to change from time to time. The early Italian masters rode single track voltes as we do today, but the eighteenth-century French masters always rode them with the haunches in. The term 'volte' has also been applied to a square pattern. The sides of the square volte were double the length of the horse. Usually these were ridden with the haunches in, because such a movement was particularly useful in hand-to-hand fighting on the battlefield.

In modern dressage competitions a single track circle of 6, 8, or 10 metres diameter is expected.

The **shallow loop** is a simple bending exercise which helps to supple the horse and flex him laterally. Because the change from one direction to the next is gradual, this gives the rider time to ensure that the horse bends correctly.

The **spiral** is a useful pattern for changing

patterns before they notice that anything is wrong.

When the horse's lateral suppleness and capacity for collection improve he will be able to negotiate a **small circle** and still maintain the appropriate degree of bending.

To discover how small a circle your horse can manage, practise several circles in succession, each one smaller than the last, until you have difficulty bending him or negotiating the pattern. Riding a few circles close to this limit will be a good exercise for the horse, but if you ride too many the exercise will be very stressful and the horse will start to evade.

You will find that your horse can negotiate a smaller circle at walk than he can at trot,

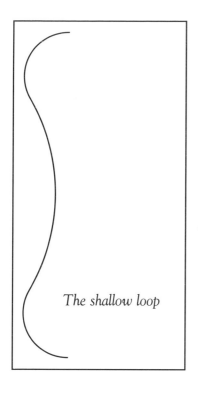

The shallow loop

The spiral

The figure of eight

the degree of the bend gradually. You can spiral both inwards and outwards.

The *figure of eight* provides an opportunity for bending the horse in both directions. The pattern should resemble two equally sized circles whose circumferences touch. Depending on the ability of your horse, the circles can be as large or as small as you wish. You will find that the hardest part of the exercise is changing the bend smoothly at the cross-over point.

The *serpentine* is a bending exercise which supples the horse laterally in both directions. A serpentine with an odd number of loops will leave you on the same rein as that from which you started.

If you ride it with straight lines separating the loops you will have plenty of time to

straighten up your horse and bend him in the opposite direction. If you ride it as a sequence of semicircles or curly loops then you will have to change the bend from left to right or vice versa much more quickly. This will be a good test of your ability to change the bend. In modern dressage competitions you are expected to ride the serpentine as semicircles joined by straight lines, but there is no reason to restrict yourself to this variation when training.

The change of bend must always appear smooth, without the horse throwing himself into the new direction. You will need to make good use of your new inside leg on the girth to activate the horse's inside hindleg as he moves into each new bend, otherwise his hindquarters will be liable to tilt over sideways. A hint of shoulder-in immediately following each

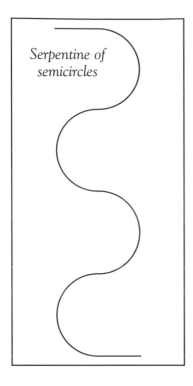

Serpentine of semicircles

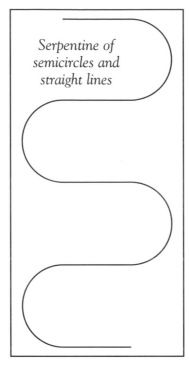

Serpentine of semicircles and straight lines

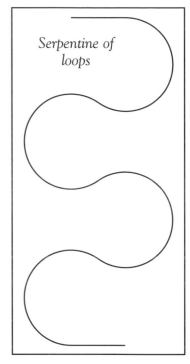

Serpentine of loops

change of bend will improve the horse's posture through the pattern.

The **square** is seldom ridden these days, presumably because it is not demanded in dressage tests. Nevertheless it is a perfectly respectable pattern which is difficult to ride accurately, and consequently it provides a good test of the rider's skill. Any size can be attempted, from the large square that occupies the whole width of the school, down to one whose sides are twice the length of the horse.

To make it easy you can ride the square with one corner in a corner of the school so that two of the sides are adjacent to the walls, or you can ride it with just one side against a wall.

The corners can be ridden as quarter voltes on a single track, but you can also ride them on two tracks with the haunches in, which will look more impressive. At walk you could ride quarter pirouettes in the corners in the direction of the turn, or three-quarter pirouettes against the direction of the turn.

As a harder alternative you could ride the entire square with the haunches-in.

Changing the rein

There are many different patterns which can be ridden to change the rein. Use all the variations you can, to add interest to your schooling. Here are some examples:

Although the **counter change of hand** is related to the change along the diagonal, it

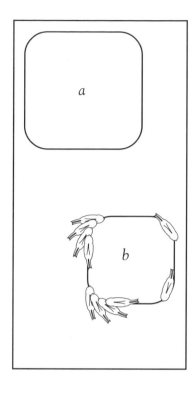

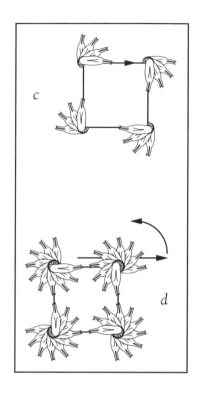

a Square in the corner of the school with single track corners.   *b* Square against the long side with internal corners ridden haunches-in.   *c* Square volte ridden at walk, with a quarter pirouette in each corner.   *d* Square volte ridden at walk with three-quarter pirouettes, against the direction of the volte, in each corner.

is not actually a change of rein at all. It consists of starting to ride a change of rein, or 'change of hand' along the diagonal, but on reaching the centre line, countering the change by returning on a diagonal track to the far corner of the wall. It keeps the horse attentive to the aids so that he does not always assume that a rein change is required as soon as he is turned onto the diagonal. It also provides an opportunity for riding two straight lines away from the track, and as such it is a good test of your own and your horse's ability to keep straight without the help of a wall.

The **reversed change of hand** is a variation

of the counter change of hand, which was designed to prevent the horse anticipating the line to the corner. Following a counter change he is turned towards the wall to change rein.

To **change the circle**, involves changing to a different circle in the opposite direction. In other words you must ride a single figure of eight, and then continue riding on the new circle.

Any **serpentine** with an even number of loops can be ridden to change the rein.

The **half volte and change** is sometimes

Single track
patterns

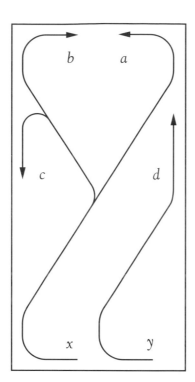

Patterns in
half-pass

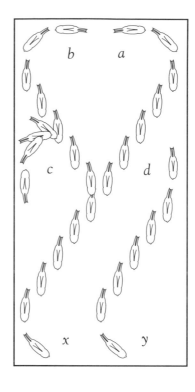

x – a *Change of rein along the diagonal*
x – b *Counter change of hand*
x – c *Reversed change of hand*
y – d *Change of rein along the short diagonal*

referred to simply as a **demi-volte**. Nowadays it is usually ridden as a single track pattern, but it can also be ridden with the haunches in.

A **change out of the corner** is a **half volte and change**, ridden in the corner.

A **change into the corner** is a **change into a half volte**, ridden in the corner.

The **half turn on the forehand** and the **half pirouette** can both be used to change direction.

The **passade** is an exercise in which the

horse traces and retraces the same path in opposite directions alongside a wall. It is an old military movement which seems to have fallen into disuse.

The turns at either end are effected by riding a demi-volte – a half volte with the haunches in and a return to the track with a short half-pass. The path along the wall can be ridden in collection or extension, but the turns must be ridden in collection. They can be as large or as small as you like, but the smaller turns are quicker and look more impressive. It is important not to lose the rhythm or the impulsion through the turns.

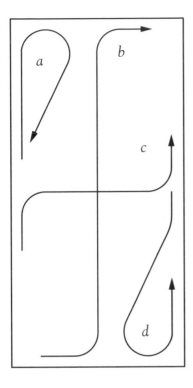

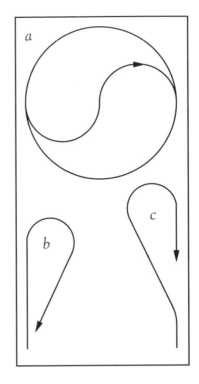

a *Change out of the corner*
b *Change down the centre line*
c *Change across the school*
d *Change into the corner*

a *Change within the circle*
b *Half volte and change*
c *Change into the half volte*

The passade can be executed at canter only by advanced horses that can perform flying changes. In the past the military were expected to turn in three strides of canter, perform a flying change, and then travel five horse's lengths before making the next turn. They either rode the straight line in collection or in the case of the 'furious passade', they started in collection and then sent the horse on at an extended canter in the second half.

Lateral movements

There are countless combinations of patterns which can be ridden to incorporate the shoulder-in, haunches-in,

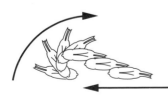
The passade
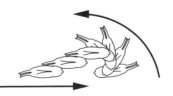

and half-pass. Every single track pattern can also be ridden laterally. There is plenty of scope for ingenuity. A few ideas are outlined below.

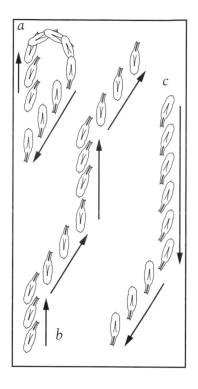

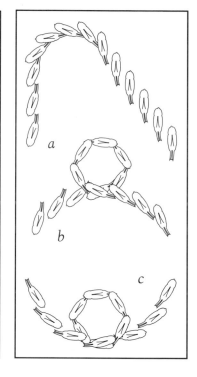

a Shoulder-in, half volte, half-pass

b Shoulder-in, half-pass, shoulder-in, half-pass

c Haunches-out, change of bend, shoulder-in, half-pass

Pattern c cannot be ridden at canter, as it is not possible to change to a shoulder-in right when cantering haunches-out on the left lead

Half volte, shoulder-in, semi-circle, half-pass, haunches-out along the wall and through the corner, shoulder-out down the centre line

a Haunches-out along the wall and on a semicircle, half-pass

b Shoulder-out, volte, haunches-out on the large circle

c Shoulder-in, volte, haunches-in on the large circle

12

COMMON PROBLEMS

Fidgeting when mounting

Potentially this is a very dangerous vice, because if the horse were to move suddenly while you were mounting up you might fall. Occasionally one meets a horse with a reputation for reacting violently when mounting up, perhaps by bucking, for example. One should always make an attempt at curing the problem rather than mounting up regardless and ignoring it.

Be careful to sit down gently in the saddle when you mount. If you bump on the horse's back he will remember it and become apprehensive and difficult on future occasions. Check that the saddle fits correctly and is not hurting him. If there is some physiological problem with his back then it will make him fearful of the mounting process if it causes him pain.

Always do your best to make the horse stand still. If necessary get an assistant to help. Placing the horse against a wall will restrict his movement considerably. You

may be able to teach him to stand still by walking him alongside the wall and bringing him to a halt from time to time. Walk him on again before he fidgets, but each time try to make him stand still for a little longer. Pat him or give him a tit-bit when he is still and calm. Repeat the procedure with the assistant half mounting and leaning across his back each time you halt. Be sure to reward the horse whenever he accepts the work calmly.

If a normally calm horse suddenly starts behaving badly when you mount up then there is usually some fairly obvious cause. Perhaps some foreign body has become lodged under the saddle, or maybe there is something close by which is upsetting him.

Horse never goes well in the manege

This is usually a problem with the rider rather than the horse. When hacking out, horses are often more enthusiastic; they enjoy the opportunity for faster motion and they can move on straight lines most of the time, which they find less tiring than circling. Their natural enthusiasm in these circumstances overcomes the setback of having to carry a poor rider.

In the school the horse will move perfectly willingly if you can conform exactly to his motion, but otherwise he will find you uncomfortable to carry, and he will be reluctant to move. The solution is to check your deportment and to learn to move as one with the horse. Probably some lunge lessons would help to improve your seat.

This problem is very common. Many riders are only prepared to ride 'hot' horses because they do not need to expend so much energy when riding them. Their riding is often so poor that they are unable to keep the colder types moving without a great deal of exertion. Hot horses invariably have more energy in reserve to overcome the inhibiting effects of their riders.

The horse has an excellent memory, and it is important that he enjoys his work in the school. Sometimes unhappy experiences from the past will adversely affect his performance.

Sometimes a horse that seems lethargic will actually have very basic problems with his deportment. If he is above the bit, or hollow in the back, for example, the energy will not transmit through his body properly and he will be unable to move freely forwards. He must be taught to relax, stretch his topline, and raise his back, and then the apparent laziness will disappear.

Laziness is a major problem with some horses. Often this can only be overcome by a rider with a strong seat and effective legs. Do not waste energy kicking away at the horse's sides if it has no effect. A smack with the whip will be a much more effective way to set him in motion, and it should be repeated every time he ignores the leg aids. If you find you are having to use the whip a great deal it might be kinder to use spurs. Try riding without stirrups. This will give you a deeper, more effective seat. If you still have difficulty then seek the advice of a more experienced rider and check that you are applying the aids correctly.

Overweight and underfed horses can both be prone to laziness. Check that the feeding regime is correct and make any necessary changes.

Horse is too spirited

Do not attempt to ride your horse if you are likely to have an accident. Calm him down first, and avoid riding him under conditions that are likely to excite him. If he has been stabled for a long time and is feeling exuberant then lunge him or turn him out in a paddock for a while before riding him. If you lunge him then aim to keep him calm and disciplined on the lunge. Never provoke him into a frenzy in the hope that it will tire him out.

When riding a particularly lively horse always stay calm and relaxed yourself. Apply your aids tactfully and never be abrupt. Spend plenty of time at the walk before moving on to the trot or the canter because the walk has a greater calming effect. Do not be tempted to take a strong contact on the reins as this will only agitate the horse and aggravate his nervousness. Talking to him quietly and stroking his neck will help to keep him steady, as will riding in the company of a quieter animal.

Always be ready to lean backwards if the horse makes a sudden move, as you will then be less likely to lose your balance.

Make sure you keep the horse's attention. He must concentrate more on you than on his surroundings. Do not try to regain his attention by hitting him. He will not notice a light tap if his mind is elsewhere, but if you hit him harder he will be surprised by it and over-react. Changes of direction can be used to regain his concentration. Keep him at the same gait for reasonably long periods without making too many transitions. Turns on the forehand and lateral movements are particularly useful: they have the advantage that they put you more in control of the haunches.

The horse should never volunteer an uninvited upward transition. He must be corrected in such a case by riding a downward transition immediately. It may help to keep him under control if you bring him to a halt before moving on again.

Many riders prefer their horses to be 'hot', and sometimes they give them more hard feed than is strictly necessary. The horse must be in a state such that you need to do something active to produce the energy output you require. If your horse has surplus energy and you are continually having to hold him back then you will not be able to school him effectively. Check his feeding regime to see if the concentrates can be reduced.

Bolting

Bolting can be caused by fear, and here the answer is to accustom the horse to the frightening object. If he cannot distance himself from it by bolting he will just keep on going. Sometimes a highly strung horse will run away because of something as commonplace as a lost stirrup dangling against his side: he should be made familiar with the feel of loose stirrups on the lunge, where no-one will come to any harm.

Sitting on a large horse bolting flat out around the manege is a very frightening experience, especially negotiating the corners with the horse leaning over as if he were going round a wall of death! If this happens to you, do not panic, do not lean forwards, but go with the horse, lean when he leans, and try to calm him down.

It is in the nature of the horse to bolt in the face of danger. He must learn to be attentive to your aids and have confidence in your judgement. If the horse ignores you and concentrates on his surroundings then he will be more likely to bolt. Frequent changes of direction will help to keep his attention. Changes of gait will also have this effect, but they will not do anything to calm him down if he is fresh. Do not be afraid to use your voice to keep the horse attentive, and remember to speak soothingly to reassure him when he is frightened. Never add to his fear by punishing him.

Some horses practise bolting as an evasion. They can bolt at canter, trot, and even at the walk! Most horses offer speed as an evasion because it is the easiest way they can avoid carrying weight properly on their haunches. Bolting is merely the same problem taken to the extreme. Horses with weak hindquarters are more likely to evade by bolting, because to them the effort of engaging the hindlegs is very uncomfortable. Such animals will need to be worked more slowly and gradually than their stronger compatriots.

Bolting horses have a knack of getting into a position from which the stopping aids have no effect. Quite often they need to brace themselves against a firm contact on the bit to achieve this effect, so the solution must involve lightening the rein contact. In particular do not take a firm contact on the horse's stiff side. When working towards the stiff side on a horse that is inclined to bolt, carry the whip on that side to keep his hindleg well engaged and try to keep a contact only on the softer outside rein.

Bucking

Your reaction to bucking should depend on its cause. A young or fresh horse who is just being exuberant should be treated more leniently than the evil monster who is deliberately trying to unseat you. The latter should be punished immediately with the whip, or spurs, and with a harsh voice. This is also one of the few occasions in riding when a jab in the mouth is in order. The horse must learn that you have dominion over him, or a very dangerous situation will arise.

How much punishment you mete out to the bucking horse will depend on circumstances. If you have a young horse, then just sitting the buck and ignoring it is a good policy, because although it does nothing to discourage the behaviour it doesn't spoil his spirit and enthusiasm for life. He will grow out of the habit as he matures.

Fortunately bucking is most often caused by excitement, and then it is not so dangerous. If you are quick enough you can prevent the buck by lifting your hands to keep the horse's head up as you feel him preparing himself for action. You should lean back well behind the vertical and then you will not be unseated. It is not a good idea to fall off: the horse will enjoy his freedom and will certainly try to do it again!

If you have a horse that is prone to bucking then ride him energetically onwards with long strides. Do not allow him to hold himself back, and do not restrict him with the reins. Restore his balance by circling rather than by taking hold of the reins, which would make him feel confined and would give him an excuse to release the energy with a buck.

If your horse does not usually buck but suddenly starts doing so, there could be a simple explanation such as a sore back or some object trapped under the saddle.

When using the schooling whip be careful where and how you apply it. Usually you will need to use it just behind your leg. If you hit too hard or too far back on the flanks, or on the quarters then you may well provoke a buck. Make sure that you do not smack a sensitive horse too hard.

Always try a very light touch first to assess the reaction. Take care that you do not carry the whip in such a position that the tip touches the horse without your realising it.

Rearing

When this happens in the manege it is usually a result of rider provocation, although it can sometimes be an evasive technique calculated to enable the horse to avoid his work. Rearing can be very dangerous because the horse may fall over backwards and cause a nasty accident. It must be prevented at all costs.

Rearing can be caused by holding an excited horse back too much with the reins. It can be provoked by pulling on the mouth, particularly on a stiff, hard-mouthed animal, and it can be caused by using a curb as a brake.

When you feel the horse preparing to rear you should cease everything you are doing immediately and be passive with your seat, legs, and hands. This will remove his motive for rearing, and will usually be sufficient to dissuade him from his intended course of action. Ride him forwards on light reins and reconsider your approach to whatever you were trying to achieve when the incident occurred.

If you keep the horse turning he will be less likely to be able to get into a position from which he can rear. If you suspect he might be preparing for another attempt then turn him sharply to one side; towards his softer side for preference. If he does lift his fore feet from the ground then lean back immediately, lighten the reins and drive him forwards strongly. Should he rise so high that you risk going over backwards you are better off leaning forwards, and slightly to one side. Turn him to one side, and he will come down again.

Learn to recognise the circumstances under which the horse rears so that you can avoid provoking this disobedience.

Refusing to move, or running backwards

If the horse resists in this way then there is always a good reason, and you must ascertain the cause so that you can understand your horse and deal with the problem.

Fear is one of the most common causes. By nature the horse is a timid creature, and any sight which seems unusual to him might be enough to initiate such a response. Coupled with weak riding or a lack of confidence in his rider's judgement, he is liable develop a habit of behaving in this way.

If your horse will not pass some frightening object, then he may lose his fear if a bolder animal approaches first. If you are alone, then take your time and approach by degrees, stroking his neck and making encouraging sounds to reassure him. If he turns away then bring him back and start again. When eventually he plucks up the courage to go past the object of his fear, be ready for him to do so at speed!

With some horses it is possible to dismount and lead them past a frightening object, as it gives them confidence if you go past first.

This is not recommended with very nervous animals in case they break away from you in panic. If you have plenty of room, as you would in the manege or in an open space, it is very helpful to circle around near the object. Gradually you will be able to move the circle closer to the object as the horse begins to realise that there is nothing to fear.

Making unreasonable demands of the horse is another common cause of this sort of resistance. If you are attempting an exercise which is too difficult for him because he is weak or inexperienced, then he will soon find ways of avoiding the effort. The answer is to make the work easier and to school him more gradually.

Horses can be very clever at avoiding work. They will sometimes try new evasions to see if they can make life easier for themselves and gain some advantage over their riders. If you really are making reasonable demands and your horse is just being difficult, then a smack with the whip or a touch of the spurs will remind him to do as he is bid.

A simple explanation for the horse running backwards could be that you are sitting badly or have too strong a contact on the reins, something which is more likely to happen when you are attempting a new exercise. Ease the tension in the reins and ride him forwards before making another attempt.

When trying new exercises do not start a fight with your horse if he runs backwards. The best course of action to take is to calm yourself and your horse down by relaxing and waiting a minute or two before attempting to move on again. When you do move on then do so at a free walk, and make a turn rather than trying to walk straight ahead. Do not tighten the reins or lean forwards or you will make it very easy for the horse to run backwards again.

The whip-shy horse

This horse is frightened of the whip and may shy away from it if you make a sudden movement with it. Changing it from one side to another could be enough to startle him and cause him to bolt. When the horse is really terrified of the whip it may be necessary to drop it to save the situation. Usually the whip-shy horse has been mistreated with the whip at some time in the past.

It is very important that the whip is never used as a punishment unless it is justly deserved. Almost always the whip should be used as an aid, when it must be applied lightly. Never under any circumstances use the whip on the horse's head.

To cure the whip-shy horse choose a time when he is calm and ask an assistant to hold him in hand. Stroke the horse gently around his shoulders with the handle of the whip, all the time stroking him with a hand at the same time, to reassure him. When he is accustomed to that, stroke his back and flanks with the handle, before progressing to his croup and legs. Finally stroke his neck and then his head. Do not force the issue if he seems worried, but feel free to offer him tit-bits as he learns to accept the whip. Teach him to accept the touch of the whip handle on both sides of his body.

The next stage is to repeat the above procedure with the main body of the whip rather than the handle. The horse will not be cured in a day, but with patience he will eventually come to realise that you mean him no harm, and he will learn that you will never use the whip without due cause.

Head tossing

Generally one checks for problems with the fit of the bridle or with the horse's teeth, and having ruled out those possibilities one jumps to the conclusion that the horse is reacting to pollen in the atmosphere. Sometimes this is indeed the answer, but another possibility is that the rider is not providing the horse with a proper contact through the reins. The rider who supplies an inconsistent contact by yielding or resisting at random is inviting

his horse to object by tossing his head about.

Keep the reins at such a length that you do not put any pressure on the horse's mouth, and keep your hands absolutely steady, if necessary by resting them on the saddle.

The horse may have formed a habit of tossing his head about deliberately so he can avoid his work. In this case fix your hands firmly in place on the saddle or on your thighs, so that he can gain no advantage from this activity. This will enable you to prevent him from dislodging your arms or your seat. You will not need to fix your hands for all time, because before long the horse will oblige by keeping his head steady, and then you will be able to carry them normally again.

A good steady contact will always help to diminish head tossing even if it is caused

If the horse tosses his head, fix your hands firmly on the saddle so he cannot dislodge your arms or your seat

105

by external environmental influences beyond your control.

Tail swishing

This is a sign of irritation or resistance. It is often caused by a rough, strong, or continuous use of the spurs. If you are wearing spurs be sure that you are not using them inadvertently without realising it. Reduce the intensity of all your aids, and check that your posture is correct.

Grinding teeth

This is another sign of resistance. It is generally accompanied by a rein contact that is too strong. Lengthen the reins, practise less demanding exercises, and the problem should disappear. Provided the schooling is progressive the horse will eventually be able to cope with the harder exercises without resistance.

The hard mouth

Although the horse's mouth can become desensitised as a result of harsh hands and rough riding, more often this condition does not indicate a problem with the mouth at all. Usually the horse holds his jaw, poll, neck, and body rigid, and lacks flexibility in the joints of his hindlegs. The mouth just happens to be the point at which the rider connects to this unyielding animal.

The problem is general stiffness, lack of balance, and in short, a lack of proper schooling. If your horse seems hard in the mouth, then introduce a systematic schooling programme starting with simple exercises to flex him both laterally and longitudinally.

Never take a strong contact on the reins yourself; keep them long enough that the horse can carry himself without your support. Do not be tempted to change to a sharper bit. If anything a milder bit would be more appropriate as it would put less pressure on the mouth.

Leaning on the bridle

This horse pushes himself relentlessly onwards with his hindlegs, but does not bend the joints sufficiently and carries too little weight on them. Leaning on the bridle is a sign of stiffness or weakness.

A good remedy is to apply half-halts to rebalance the horse and slow him down. Use your lower legs at the same time, to increase the engagement of his hindlegs. Having obtained some improvement, yield the reins so that the horse is unable to support himself on them.

One should always, with every horse, yield the reins slightly, one after the other in the rhythm of the movement as the shoulder on each side advances. This is particularly important with the horse who likes to lean on the bit, as it will prevent him from taking a firm contact.

Occasionally one meets a horse who has discovered that he can deliberately evade the aids for engaging his hindlegs by forcing his head downwards and keeping the weight on his shoulders. Attempts at using the legs and seat to raise his head and neck are unsuccessful. The horse behaves in this way to avoid the effort of working correctly. Probably he has some weakness which makes correct work seem very tiring. He must be worked slowly and methodically, and should be given plenty of rest periods; but before schooling can commence steps must be taken to overcome the immediate difficulty.

This is one of the very few occasions when an active use of the snaffle is in order. Whilst applying your legs strongly to drive the hindlegs forwards you must raise your hands to encourage the horse to lift up his head. You may also need to tap with the whip to activate his hindquarters. Having used the reins in this way it is important that you relax the pressure again immediately and practise some exercise that will encourage the hindlegs to engage a little more. Spiralling in from a large circle to a smaller one would be a simple example. Do not keep a strong pressure on the reins to hold the head up, as the horse must learn to carry it himself.

Pulling

Either you are trying to ride with the reins too short, when because of his stage of training the horse is entitled to a long rein, or he is trying to give himself longer reins to avoid having to work in collection.

You do not need short reins or a strong contact to ride a horse. Give him the length of rein that is appropriate for his degree of collection. You should be able to ride any horse in an uncollected way with long reins. Learn to ride more with your

seat and legs so you do not feel the need to rely on the rein contact to stay in control. You will learn a valuable lesson if you practise riding downward transitions without increasing the tension in the reins.

Lengthen the reins until the horse no longer pulls, and then when you wish to collect him use the school patterns and exercises rather than your aids, to set him more on his haunches. When he becomes more collected his frame will shorten, and you will then be able to shorten the reins a little without any fear of his leaning on the bit.

If your reins are the correct length but the horse continually plunges his nose forwards to make them longer, then it is your provision of an incorrect contact that allows him to act in this way. He should never be able to dislodge your arms, and he should not be able to pull you out of the saddle. You must be ready to lean back and fix your elbows by your sides so that nothing gives when the horse plunges his head forwards. He should merely bang his jaw against the bit, and that should be sufficient to persuade him to give up the habit.

Always keep the contact light, and see if you can make it even lighter by yielding the reins to encourage the horse to work in self-carriage so that he does not rely on the bit. He should not depend on the contact to hold himself in the proper frame, but should remain balanced because of the engagement of his hindlegs. Do not try to compress him between your legs and hands in an attempt to influence the way he holds himself. This sort of tension is enormously detrimental to good riding and it will limit the amount of progress you can expect to make with your horse.

Lameness

If your horse really is lame then obviously no form of schooling will effect a cure, and you should not be riding him. However, some irregularities of gait are caused by so-called 'bridle lameness', which does not involve a physiological dysfunction. In such cases the uneven action is due to rider interference.

With bridle lameness, the problem will usually disappear if the rider lengthens the reins, and it will always disappear if the horse is trotted up in hand. There is no cause for alarm, and the horse is fit for work.

In cases where the reins are held too short, the restriction prevents the trotting horse from impacting both feet of each diagonal on the ground at exactly the same instant, and this causes him to nod his head. Lengthening the reins will effect a cure.

Sometimes the problem arises when you succeed in persuading the horse to load his hind limbs evenly, which he finds difficult because of one-sidedness. Here the uneven gait will improve with time, provided that the schooling is planned so as to even up the muscular development of the hind limbs.

Another common irregularity at trot occurs if the horse is keen to move off in canter. Every few strides he makes a half-hearted attempt at a canter transition but then falls back into a trot. Again this is not a true lameness, and the problem will disappear when the horse relaxes.

Crooked halts

During the first year of his training it is quite sufficient if the young horse manages to remain calm and stand still when he is asked to halt. By the time he has learned to stop directly from a trot, which he ought to be able to do in his second year, he is ready to learn to stand square, with neither forefoot nor hindfoot more advanced than its partner. In fact it is much easier to produce a square halt from a trot than it is from a walk.

To ensure that the horse develops the habit of standing properly at the halt always check by feel, or by glancing down, to see if he is correct. Never move on again or dismount without making the necessary corrections. You must be diligent about this or the horse will habitually halt badly.

Occasionally a horse will stop with one foreleg more advanced than the other. Although this is unusual it is a far worse fault than having one hindleg in advance of the other. It shows either that he was badly out of balance when he came to rest, or that because he has never been corrected he has developed the habit of halting badly.

The correction both for the hindlegs and for the forelegs involves moving the retarded leg forwards until it is level with its neighbour. As the horse should always develop the habit of moving forwards, it would be unwise to move the other limb backwards.

It is relatively straightforward to advance a retarded hindleg: tap your leg by the girth on the required side and he will lift the foot on that side and reposition it. Be ready to prevent him walking on if he should make a wrong guess at your intentions. You will have to repeat the correction if the repositioning is unsuccessful. Should the aid with your leg produce no response at all, then you must teach the horse to lift the leg when required. This you can do by tapping with the same leg and allowing him to walk on. Stroke his neck as a reward as he lifts the leg. Before long he will learn that the aid with your leg is an instruction for him to lift his leg, and you will be able to achieve the required result without having to walk on.

To reposition a retarded foreleg takes a little more practice, but it is easy once the knack is learned. As with the hindleg, apply your leg on the side to be moved. At the same time yield the rein on that side, and keep the contact on the other. Also at the same time apply the aids for a half-halt, i.e. tighten your abdomen and close your thighs against the saddle, in order to prevent any forward movement. Sit with your weight supported slightly more to the side of the horse's correctly placed foreleg. It may help if you tap him lightly with the whip on the shoulder of the retarded limb. Usually the horse will guess your intention quite easily because he will feel uncomfortable in the incorrect position anyway.

If you know your horse can halt properly, then a suitable punishment for those times when he does not, is to make the positional correction and then to repeat the transition, several times if necessary, until he volunteers a correct halt, at which point he should be allowed to walk on a loose rein as a reward. When he discovers that a good halt is followed by a rest he will soon learn to halt correctly every time.

Losing your stirrups

If you are inclined to lose your stirrups, particularly at the faster paces, it could simply be that they are too long, or it could indicate that you have not yet developed a sufficiently adhesive seat. If your sitting trot is not perfect, for example, you will tend to bounce up and down in the saddle, and this will be enough to lighten the grip of your feet on the stirrup irons.

Poorly developed neck muscles

With experience one can predict fairly accurately what a strange horse will be like to ride, just by looking at his muscle development. When the horse has been trained correctly the muscles along the top of his neck will be firm and well developed, whilst those on the underside will be slack.

Sometimes one finds horses whose lower neck muscles are thick and bulging whilst their upper ones are weedy and show unattractive-looking hollows below the crest. If this is the case with your horse then it is a sure sign that his deportment is incorrect. This is not necessarily your fault; it could well have been caused by a previous rider.

In order to effect a cure you will need to ride the horse on a long rein for some time, probably for two or three months. The only objective during this period must be to encourage him to stretch forwards with his neck, and downwards with his nose so that he raises his back and starts to use the

Horse with bulging lower neck muscles

Ride the horse on a long rein to develop the upper neck muscles

muscles in the top of his neck. Do not shorten up the reins or you will only allow him to stiffen up, lean on the bit, and prop his head up on the lower neck muscles.

Ride plenty of turns and circles in rising trot keeping a contact on the inside rein. Sometimes yield the outside rein and stroke the horse's crest with your outside fist to encourage him to relax, to flex to the inside, and to stretch forwards. Occasionally yield the inside rein and see if the horse

110

follows down with his head.

No two horses will react in exactly the same way, so you will have to discover which exercises or actions are the most effective in bringing about the desired results, and make ample use of those.

At first the horse will stretch down only momentarily and then return to his usual faulty position. You must reward him every time he makes the slightest indication of stretching and relaxing in the proper manner. Your job is to teach him that the correct position is the most comfortable one, and gradually to increase the length of time that he stays in this position until it becomes the norm.

Working the horse on the lunge can also be very helpful. It is important that the side-reins are kept long so that he can stretch forwards and work in a long frame.

Eventually the horse will begin to build up the muscles in the top of his neck, and you will then be free to move on to other schooling objectives.

Horse on the forehand

This horse has a very fundamental fault in the way he moves. Essentially he carries too much weight on his shoulders and too little on his haunches. Usually he takes short strides with his hindlegs, and finds lateral flexion difficult on account of stiffness in the joints of his hind limbs.

If the problem has only just been brought to your attention through a dressage score sheet or by discussion with another rider,

for example, then you are unlikely to be able to effect a cure by yourself. You would be well advised to ride some horses that move correctly so that you become familiar with the proper feeling, otherwise you will not understand what the objectives are. It will probably be necessary to engage the services of a more experienced rider to re-school your horse.

The remedy will include circling at trot, encouraging the horse to take longer strides whilst working on a long rein so that his back is unrestricted. Shortening the reins to hold his head up would be counter-productive because it would interfere with the engagement of the hindlegs. When circling, the rider's inside rein, inside seat, and inside leg will be more effective than the outside aids at improving the lateral bending and the engagement of the inside hindleg.

Hollowing the back

This problem can arise if a young horse is backed too early by a rider that is too heavy, and it can be aggravated by a weak back, poor conformation, or clumsy riding, particularly if the rider sits too far back in the saddle or bounces on the horse's back. It cannot be caused by a rider who sits deeply in the saddle and knows how to absorb the motion in his lower back.

A hollow back is invariably accompanied by a lack of engagement of the hindlegs. Sometimes it is offered by the horse as an evasion, in which case you must be particularly attentive to the engagement and apply your legs and seat as necessary so that the problem cannot arise.

In more chronic cases the problem cannot be cured without first removing the cause. Only then can the horse's back can be strengthened by putting him through a course of lungeing and then riding for short periods, working particularly on encouraging him to engage his hindlegs, to take long strides, and to lower his head and raise his back.

Where the problem is caused by bad riding the rider must be reeducated and taught to sit correctly, preferably by means of lunge lessons on a horse with a strong back.

Leaning onto one shoulder

This is an evasion caused by crookedness. The horse holds himself in such a position that you cannot make him use his haunches properly.

For the horse that leans onto the left shoulder, circle him to the right holding the right rein, and yield the pressure on the left rein. Do not take a firm hold of the left rein to straighten him up, because although this will shift the weight away from the left shoulder, it will not provide a long term solution: the horse would merely collapse to the right again as soon as you released the pressure on the left rein. He must be straightened by persuading him to take more weight on his right hindleg.

Keep your right seatbone pressed well down into the saddle and use your right leg on the girth to encourage the right hindleg to work harder. Riding in a shoulder-fore position to the right will give you a better chance of being able to place the right hind foot in the required position on the ground.

When turning to the left, if the horse counter-flexes to the right and leans onto his left shoulder you will have to take a contact on the left rein to assist with reestablishing the left bend, but release the pressure as soon as you can and encourage the horse to take a contact on the right rein. If you then change to a shoulder-in left position it will help the horse to shift his weight over towards his right shoulder.

From this position you could test the success of your strategy by asking for a left lead canter, or by changing to a haunches-in exercise to the left. Both of these alternatives would be difficult for the horse if he were still leaning towards his left shoulder. Incidentally they would also both help to strengthen the weaker right hindleg.

Stiffness

Some horses start their work more stiffly than others. They should be given a longer period of limbering up before their proper schooling begins. Plenty of walk on a long rein and some lateral work at a collected walk will often help. Lungeing for a few minutes before riding may help to loosen up particularly stiff animals.

With many horses a short canter will alleviate stiffness more effectively than work at the trot. Older horses will often find the canter easier than the trot, provided of course that the working surface is suitable and that they have a reasonably balanced canter.

Keep the horse in a long frame while you

loosen him up so that he can relax his back. You will be able to work towards collection after you have practised some lengthening strides, which will free his joints and enable him to move with more elasticity.

A stiff horse deserves a supple rider. He will stiffen himself up all the more if he has an uncomfortable load to carry.

Some horses, although not naturally stiff, hold themselves rigid as a deliberate ploy to avoid their work. It is almost impossible to bend these horses laterally, and it feels as though they have a metal rod running all the way from poll to tail.

The solution to this problem involves practising lateral flexions of the horse's neck and poll. Working at a halt, make the horse turn his head left and right alternately. This will probably be more difficult than it sounds. Since he is holding himself rigidly, any attempt to turn his head to the right will almost certainly result in him remaining absolutely straight and moving his croup out to the left. A similar difficulty will arise when attempting to bend his neck to the left. In order to succeed with the bending, repeatedly give and take on a fairly short inside rein and use your outside leg behind the girth to prevent the croup from moving. Reward the horse as soon as he bends, by yielding the reins.

Having succeeded in flexing the neck right and left at the halt, the next step is to convince the horse that he can move without holding himself rigidly. Ask him to walk on while his neck is bent to one side, and then repeat with it bent in the other

direction. If you then try a few steps of trot with the neck bent you will find that the horse relaxes his back much more than usual, and he will probably lower his head and round his neck very quickly. You must reduce the amount of bend in the neck without delay. It would not be correct to work the horse in an over-bent lateral position. The strategy is merely a short term expedient to show the horse that he is able to move without locking his neck muscles in one position. You will probably need to repeat the remedy from time to time over several schooling sessions before the cure becomes permanent.

The type of horse that tries this rigid evasion technique is often impetuous, but has rather weak hindquarters which he does not like to use for weight support. He likes to rush around out of control. Take care to increase the schooling demands very gradually so as not to overwork his weak limbs. In other words avoid provoking the resistance.

Counter-flexing

If the horse is turning towards his stiff side and is bent in the opposite direction it could just be a sign of crookedness. However, the problem sometimes arises as a result of inattentiveness on the part of both horse and rider. Even if the horse does have one very stiff side any rider should be able to bend him to some extent in both directions.

Check that your posture corresponds to the bend you require, i.e. your outside leg is further back than your inside leg, and your shoulders are turned towards the

Counter-flexed horse on the right rein, but looking to the left

To help the horse to bend to the right, rest your right hand on the saddle and stroke his neck with your left fist

direction of travel.

Notice how your horse is bending. Do not allow him to look around and gaze at the scenery on the outside of the bend. If he is difficult to bend in the correct direction then rest your inside hand on the saddle and stroke his neck with your outside fist. This will help him to turn his head to the inside.

114

Cutting corners

This generally means the horse is not yet strong enough to negotiate tight turns. You will have to be content with large arcs through the corners until his hindlegs become strong enough that the inside one can support him around curves of a smaller radius.

Do not try to force the horse into the corner with your outside rein. This will not help in the long term as it will do nothing to strengthen his inside hindleg. It is more important to keep him properly bent and balanced through whatever size of turn he can manage comfortably.

If the horse habitually anticipates the corners and cuts in, modify his turn and guide him around a small circle and back to the wall again. He will soon realise that whenever he cuts in he has to work harder, and before long he will stop doing it.

Horse will not canter

The problem could be that you are not applying the aids correctly, that you are not preparing the horse properly for the transition, or that once in canter you are unable to conform to the motion of his back. In the latter case he will find the gait too uncomfortable, and will very quickly revert to a trot.

If your riding skills are satisfactory but the horse has previously been ridden by a poor rider then he may refuse to canter because he is expecting it to be uncomfortable. A smack or two with the stick will set him into canter the first time. He will then discover that it is quite comfortable after all, and next time he will canter more willingly.

Some horses will try to rush forwards in trot as an evasion when they are asked to canter. They do this because it requires less effort. Practise some exercises to put the horse more onto his haunches before you attempt the canter. A half-halt might be all that is required, or you could ride a few trot to halt and halt to trot transitions, for example. Another good preparation would be to ride a half turn on the forehand before moving off at a trot and asking for a canter straight away.

If you are still unsuccessful then try lungeing the horse to see how easily he canters. If he genuinely does find it difficult to balance himself at canter then he should learn to perfect the gait unmounted before he masters it under the saddle.

Horse will canter on one lead only

Be particularly careful to apply the aids correctly when asking for a canter on the more difficult lead. Exaggerate the position of your outside leg by taking it farther back than usual. Bend the horse in the direction of the required lead before attempting the canter and do not let him lean towards his inside shoulder. A few turns around the forehand away from your inside leg may help to bend him in the proper direction and shift his weight towards his outside shoulder. Keep the contact on the inside rein as you issue the aid for canter, and yield the outside rein, to help maintain the bend to the inside.

If you over-shorten the horse or have too much tension in the reins the problem will get worse. Work him on a long rein so he can relax. Ride a few circles at a trot in both directions and ask for a canter when the horse seems relaxed and you are circling in the direction of the required lead. The cross-over point of a figure of eight is an excellent place to strike off into canter. Ask for the transition immediately after changing the bend towards the difficult side.

Another strategy is to ask for the canter as you ride through a corner of the manege, where it would be harder for the horse to produce a false canter on his favourite lead. If you approach the corner on a slanting line so you have to turn through an acute angle as you ask for the canter you will increase your chances of producing a correct strike-off. A low angled pole leaning across the corner may help too. Ask for the canter as the horse hops over it.

To make it hard for the horse to lead with his favourite leg try riding a shoulder-in towards the required lead, and as you ask for canter keep the bend but change direction and guide him in the direction in which his nose is pointing, so that he starts the canter in a haunches-in position. This is liable to produce a crooked canter, which you must then straighten; but at least it is better than no canter at all or a false canter. This method should not be used once the horse has discovered how to canter on the difficult lead.

When you succeed in producing a canter

on the more difficult lead keep the horse cantering for a short distance, all the time stroking his neck and praising him, and then allow him to walk as a reward.

Horse lifts his head when striking off into canter

The reason the horse raises his head is to lighten his shoulders so that he can perform the transition more easily. Instead he should take the weight back by engaging his hindlegs.

A good correction is to press your inside hand against the saddle as you ask for the canter transition so that it cannot be dislodged. This will deny the horse the opportunity of lifting up his head. The engagement of the inside hindleg can be improved if the horse is given a shoulder-fore position before striking off into canter.

Disunited canter

This occurs as a result of an unbalanced transition. Horses are more often disunited in front, leading with the incorrect foreleg, but they do sometimes lead with the incorrect hindleg.

Sometimes the canter can be corrected merely by repeating the aids at each stride and waiting for the horse to change the incorrect pair of legs. This is easier if you are turning in the direction of the required lead rather than riding straight ahead.

The easiest solution is to change back to a trot or a walk, rebalance the horse, and start another canter.

Hind feet insufficiently separated at canter

This horse places his hind feet almost side by side on the ground at canter and appears not to have a leading hindleg. This gait impurity can be caused by working too much in collection, or by attempting to collect the horse beyond his capability. A good cure is to practise lengthening and shortening strides at canter.

Unbalanced canter

When hacking out, most riders walk or trot whenever they feel like it, but do not have the same nonchalant attitude to the canter. The usual reason is that whilst they are totally in control at walk and trot, at canter they cease riding, become passengers, and allow their horses to produce a canter of their own devising. Eventually when they are ready to return to trot they have a struggle to wrest back some control before they can bring about the transition.

This is not the way to ride the canter. You must be in control of every stride that the horse takes. It is far too dangerous to become a passenger when riding such a strong and naturally dominant animal as the horse. Whenever you feel you are getting out of control use a half-halt to rebalance the horse. If you are not confident that the half-halt is effective, then check your control periodically by coming back to a trot or a walk, and then ask for another canter. The horse must not be allowed to dictate anything about the gait; you must decide whether he is to move at a collected canter, a working

canter, or any other sort of canter.

There is no need for the canter to be a fast gait. When riding in company you should be able to ride a collected canter quite easily alongside another horse that is trotting. If your horse is proficient at collection you might even be able to canter slowly beside a horse that is walking. Provided you make no change in speed you should be able to ride the gait of your choice without upsetting another horse.

Make frequent use of the walk to canter transition and you will find that you can achieve a more collected and hence a more controlled canter.

Practising lengthening and shortening strides at canter will help to improve the horse's balance. You will find that circles and spirals will assist with the engagement of his hindlegs and will help to produce a more controlled canter.

Haunches fall in at canter

This is one of the most common signs of crookedness. The horse moves in this way so that he can avoid the effort of carrying the proper amount of weight on his inside hindleg.

One correction would be to ride a small circle and one step of the next circle and then to move straight ahead in a shoulder-fore position. You may be able to effect a correction without riding the circle, by taking just one or two steps on a circular track and then proceeding in the shoulder-fore position.

Alternatively, bring the horse's forehand one or two steps inwards using both reins and your outside leg, until his shoulders are positioned directly in front of the evading hindleg. This correction will bring the horse away from his original track, but that is unimportant.

You may find it easier to keep the horse straight in counter-canter.

Canter is followed by a jolting trot

This is a sign of a poorly balanced canter. You can improve the trot which follows the canter by working on the preparation for the transition. Before asking the horse to trot use a half-halt to collect him, and ride on a circle rather than a straight line, as this will make it easier to engage the hindlegs.

Practise several canter to trot transitions, each time collecting the trot and then striking off into canter again after a few strides. Ride only a few canter strides before attempting the next transition to trot. Sometimes, instead of changing to a trot, just apply a half-halt and allow the horse to continue in canter on a light rein. This canter will be more collected and better balanced, and the next transition to trot should show some improvement.

Make sure you can conform to the motion of the horse's back at canter, and check that you are correctly applying the aids for the trot transition. If you use too much rein pressure this could cause the horse to fall into an uncontrolled trot.

Head and neck swing to and fro at walk and canter

When the horse moves in this way it is a sign that he is not using his back and hindquarters correctly. He moves stiffly without bending and taking the strain on the joints of his hindlegs. He compensates for this stiffness by swinging his head and neck backwards and forwards to keep himself in balance.

Do not move your arms back and forwards, or the horse will only continue to move badly. Hold them still, but keep the reins long enough that they will not restrict the horse. When he tries to stretch his head forwards and finds he cannot do so because of the steady rein contact he will seek another way of moving to keep himself in balance. He will very soon start to use his back and hindlegs correctly.

This problem is easier to cure if you work on exercises which improve the collection. Turns on the forehand at walk, and spiralling inwards onto a small circle at trot or canter will help to exercise the hind limbs and make it easier for the horse to discover how to use them correctly.

Lungeing in side-reins will also help to improve the way the horse moves.

Horse cannot sustain the counter-canter

It is possible that the horse is not yet ready for this exercise. You may have to work more on the lateral movements and the direct transitions to make him sufficiently strong, supple, and collected. When you attempt the counter-canter do not be too ambitious: ride only very shallow loops at first, and turn away in the direction of the leading leg before the horse breaks to a trot.

Sometimes the rider's aiding is at fault. Keep the horse bent towards the side of his leading leg, and keep your outside leg well back behind the girth. Drive through the inside of your seat at every stride.

Horse gouges channels when reining back

The horse drags his feet when reining back, instead of lifting them up and stepping back. This can be caused by too strong a rein contact, which the rider will be tempted to apply if the horse is reluctant to move backwards. The contact should be a passive resistance but not a pull.

When teaching the movement ask an assistant to push the horse back rather than pulling on the reins. If you lean further forwards you will find the horse moves more easily. A tap with the whip will encourage him to step more smartly.

Horse will not rein back in a straight line

This is a sign of crookedness. It is the result of an uneven use of the hind limbs. Usually the haunches deviate towards the hollow side because the hindleg on that side is weaker and tends to give way when it takes the weight. If your schooling programme takes account of crookedness as it should, by practising exercises which strengthen

the weaker hindleg, then the problem will diminish in due course.

When the horse is learning to rein back it is always hard for him to keep straight. It will be much easier for him if you practise alongside a wall.

If the horse does step out of line you will find that you are very limited in the corrective measures you can take with your legs. The best strategy is to keep his shoulders directly in front of his haunches. If he moves his quarters to the right, for example, then use both reins to take his shoulders over to the right by the same amount, or perhaps a little more. At the same time bend the horse a little to the left. In this way the backward thrust from the shoulders will help to send him in the required direction.

Speedy extensions

The horse changes rhythm, increasing the frequency of his footfalls, and runs faster instead of lengthening his stride and keeping to the same rhythm. This is the typical reaction of a horse who carries too much weight on his shoulders or who cannot bend the joints of his hindlegs sufficiently.

The tendency to speed up can be reduced by preparing the horse for the extension by getting him more onto his haunches. A half-halt may be all that is required, but to get even better extensions try riding a volte in collection, or a shoulder-in or a half-pass as a preparation. When extending the stride the horse's hip joints become more active. Because the half-pass exercises the hips this lateral movement is a particularly effective preparation.

Sometimes a horse will stiffen his back and lift his head above the bit when he is asked to extend. First encourage him to stretch his head and neck forwards and down, and then choose a moment when it is moving downwards to drive him on. If he lifts his head again then slow him down and encourage him to relax before sending him forwards again. Your seat is responsible for dictating the rhythm and must act in a restraining way if the horse tries to speed up.

To extend the trot on a novice horse, a useful strategy is to utilise the canter to produce plenty of energy, and then to change to a trot and extend the stride. The extra impulsion will be quite noticeable and the horse will bound forwards with much more enthusiasm than usual.

Advanced horses can be prepared by riding a few steps of piaffe or passage, and then quite astonishing extensions are possible.

Jogging

This is an annoying habit which some horses delight in exhibiting when they ought to be walking. The worst thing to do is to allow it to continue, because like all habits it is difficult to cure. As soon as the horse tries to jog you should do something about it. You could bring him to a halt for a moment and then ask him to walk on again, for example.

To be really successful at preventing the jog trot you need to have a deep seat which

is strong enough in its influence over the horse's back to make jogging a difficult option for him to take. Half-halts or full halts will help to increase your influence over his back, and if they are applied as soon as he breaks into a jog they will act as an object lesson to him because he will find that alternating between the jog and the halt is more tiring than walking properly.

Another way to make the jog more difficult for the horse is to turn him into a shoulder-in position. You can straighten him up again as soon as he starts to walk properly again.

When you do succeed in persuading the horse to walk, encourage him to take long strides by giving him a long rein so that he can stretch well forwards and swing his back. Ride a free walk on a long rein whenever you can.

Fore foot remains on the ground at turn on the forehand

This occurs when the horse is not ridden forwards. It is a serious fault because the purity of the walk is lost. The solution is to make the horse walk forwards a little as he moves around the turn. At every step the inside forefoot should land a few inches in front of its previous position on the ground.

Hind foot remains on the ground at turn on the haunches

This is another problem caused by lack of forward progression. Use your inside leg on the girth at every stride to keep the inside hind foot stepping in rhythm. If you insist that the horse always steps forwards a little with his inside hindleg then he will be unable to perform the exercise without lifting it.

Horse moves towards rider's leg instead of away from it

This resistance sometimes occurs when teaching the horse to move laterally. It can arise when teaching the haunches-in, which is considerably more difficult for the horse than the shoulder-in. The reason for the resistance is that the inside hindleg is unable to bend to support the weight, and acts instead as an inflexible strut. The cure is to return to the shoulder-in, and spend more time on this exercise before attempting the haunches-in again.

If the horse moves towards the leg when attempting the shoulder-in, then go back a stage in his training and practise some turns on the forehand, where you will be able to exert a stronger influence over the direction in which he moves.

Head tilts at half-pass

Instead of remaining upright when viewed from the front, the horse's nose tilts towards the direction in which he is moving. The cause is a combination of weakness in the horse's inside hindleg, which does not carry enough weight to support him in the proper frame, and too much pressure on the inside rein.

To cure this problem release the pressure on the inside rein. Also check that your aids are correct: keep your outside leg back, press your inside leg well down, and support your weight more towards the inside than the outside of your seat. Sit upright rather than leaning to one side.

Changing to a shoulder-in will help to correct the horse's position and encourage the inside hindleg to engage properly. Alternating between a few steps of shoulder-in and a few steps of half-pass is a very good exercise for improving the horse's proficiency at the half-pass.

Head tilts outwards at shoulder-in

Tilting the head in this direction is indicative of a weakness in the outside hindleg, which does not carry sufficient weight.

Use a stronger outside leg, or tap on the outside with the schooling whip to encourage the hindleg on that side to work harder.

CONCLUSION

The art of riding has been practised since the days of antiquity. In former times the life of man was closely bound up with the lives of his horses. Having well trained animals to ride was indispensable, and this led to the acquisition of a wealth of knowledge about schooling the horse. Nowadays our journey through life does not depend on the quality or ability of our horses. They enhance our leisure time, but they no longer perform an essential function, so the driving forces behind our riding and training are somewhat different.

Man is by nature a competitive creature who likes to prove he is better than the next man. We live in a world of examinations and competitions, which we use to demonstrate our prowess, and to enhance our standing in society. We are seldom content with the product of our own efforts unless we are praised by others. Provided somebody is there to tell us we are the best then we are satisfied. Under these conditions we ride to impress our judges. This situation is not always healthy for the art of riding.

Often riders are so concerned with the outward appearance or 'outline' of their horses that they forget the fundamental necessities which were considered so important in the past. The old masters did not like to ride tense horses on a strong contact; but that does not seem to worry some dressage competitors, who are happy so long as their horses adopt a rounded outline and move energetically forwards.

One might imagine that knowledge about schooling the horse would survive and flourish when we are guided by experienced professionals and judges. Indeed one would have no cause for concern whatsoever, were it not for the fact that a number of the masters of bygone centuries took the trouble to publish and disseminate their contemporary knowledge of horsemanship.

The underlying tone of some of the old books is very interesting. The piaffe, for example, is mentioned in passing as if it would be ridden by anyone at any time. There is nothing to suggest that it was considered in any way difficult or out of the ordinary. Another casual comment advises the rider not to allow his horse to rise in front when halting. Today the reader would probably wonder why the author bothered with this piece of advice. Very few riders will ever find themselves in a situation where there is the remotest likelihood of the horse lifting his forefeet from the ground when halting.

One is drawn to the conclusion that our predecessors had a very different experience of riding than the average rider does today. One major difference is that they knew how to collect their horses by bending the joints of their hindlegs and setting them on their haunches. In the twentieth century we are losing this ability. The late classical riding master Nuno Oliviera made a telling observation at his last clinic in England, when he informed his audience that not one of the horses appearing during the day had been collected; and that included a number working at advanced level.

Another modern development is a new interpretation of the term 'forward'. The original meaning was literal: every step the horse takes, except when reining back, must gain a little ground to the front. Nowadays this simple meaning has been forgotten, and the instruction 'ride your horse forward' is often misinterpreted as an excuse for speed. Fast forward movement effectively removes the possibility of engaging the haunches. If only we trained our horses to move forward and upward we would get a better result.

When explaining how to ride, equestrian authors and riding instructors often base their advice on the dubious assumption that the horse has been started correctly, and has no fundamental problems. In real life this ideal situation does not occur very often. Horses and riders alike rarely have the advantage of a thorough basic education, and this adds to the difficulties encountered when embarking on a programme of schooling. The unfortunate pupil is usually expected to achieve results by applying methods that were originally developed by experienced masters when training advanced school horses. This is rather unfair, and as a compensation three concessions should be allowed when the average rider is schooling the average horse. Unfortunately these concessions are not always condoned by riding teachers.

Firstly, because they are so concerned that riders should not provide a harsh contact and fix the horse's head in place, teachers usually insist that the hands are carried in an idealised position a few inches above the pommel of the saddle. When riding a horse that is not flexing at the poll or working correctly through his topline, however, it is almost impossible to provide a contact that is steady enough to cure this problem unless one or both hands are rested against the saddle. A fixed contact is only detrimental if the reins are too short. If it were generally a bad thing then it would not be acceptable to lunge the horse in side reins. By contrast, an unsteady contact, which often occurs when the hands are carried in the 'correct' position, is always detrimental to the horse.

Secondly, because they are so worried that riders might get 'behind the movement', instructors usually disapprove of inclining the upper body behind the vertical. In practice, the act of leaning backwards can greatly increase the effectiveness of the seat. Until the seat has been perfected and the horse has learned to respond correctly to the aids, this action should be allowed provided it produces the desired response. There is nothing to be gained from remaining upright in the correct position with an ineffective seat, because it will only oblige riders to control their horses with the only other means at their disposal, namely the reins. This will not be conducive to good riding, and it will cause more schooling problems than it solves.

Thirdly, the popular concept of riding the horse between the inside leg and the outside rein is not fully understood by the average instructor, who expects this sophisticated idea to be applied to all horses regardless of how well they have been trained. The technique has no beneficial effect on novice horses. In the early stages of schooling the influence of the inside rein is far more important than that of the outside rein, because it gives the horse a point of reference that enables him to bend laterally and to stretch longitudinally at the same time.

Before you commence schooling your horse attend to your own posture and check that your riding skills are adequate for the task ahead. When you start, aim to produce a horse that is a real pleasure to ride. Keeping him relaxed and supple should be at the top of your list of priorities. Always allow him to move freely, and make sure he enjoys his work. Whenever you attempt a difficult exercise take care that he remains in a pure walk, trot, or canter, and see that the rhythm of the movement remains constant. If you get into difficulties and find you are resorting to force, then rethink your strategy, because you must be doing something wrong. You must seek to understand the cause of the problem and try to find a more gentle way of explaining your requirements to the horse.

The real fun of riding begins with collection, but you will never learn to collect your horse unless you first master the lateral exercises. It is usually better to practise these before you start the direct transitions or the counter-canter. None of these exercises is as difficult to learn as you might imagine. You will find they unlock the door to a new world of greater enjoyment for you and your horse.

Most horses move in a splendid fashion when they are free in the paddock. The real problem with riding is not so much one of training the horse, but more one of inspiring him to perform well at a time when his natural instincts are not firing him into action. Success at schooling depends partly on knowledge and experience, but it also depends on how adept you are at using the aids as a language to communicate the required message to the horse, and upon how you react when the horse misunderstands or is unable or unwilling to comply with your wishes. In short it requires empathy with the horse.

BIBLIOGRAPHY

Alois Podhajsky
The Complete Training of Horse and Rider
Harrap, London, 1967
(ISBN 0 245 59040 4)

This book, written by a former director of the Spanish Riding School in Vienna, gives a thorough explanation of how the horse should be trained in the classical manner.

Charles de Kunffy
The Athletic Development of the Dressage Horse
Macmillan Publishing Co., New York and London, 1992
(ISBN 0 87605 896 9)

A book containing a great variety of schooling ideas, with many insights into how the riding horse can be brought to his full athletic potential, written by a leading classical riding master.

Eleanor Ross
School Exercises for Flatwork and Jumping
Kenilworth Press, Bucks, 1992
(ISBN 1 872082 31 9)

An excellent handbook presented by an experienced riding teacher and trainer, which describes, with the help of diagrams, a large number of schooling patterns and exercises.

INDEX

126

F